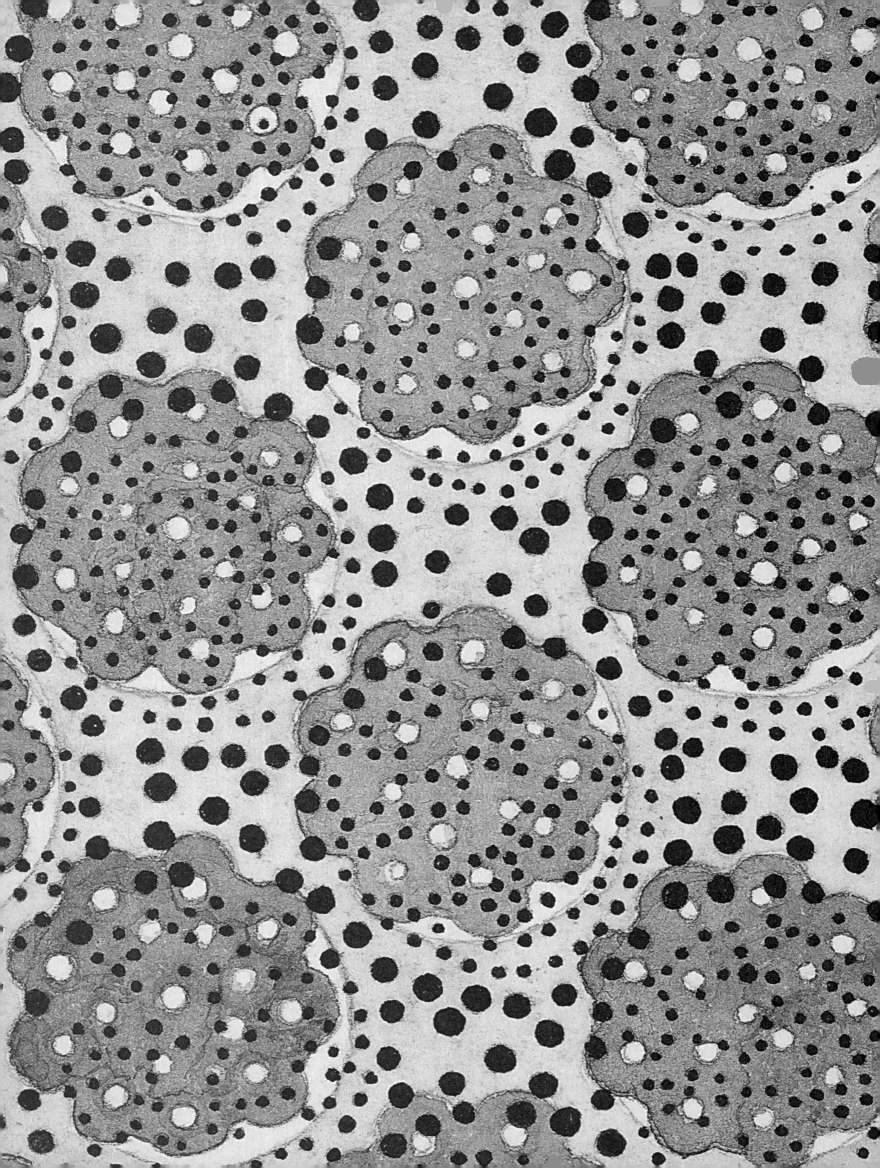

WALLPAPER
A HISTORY OF STYLE AND TRENDS

CAROLLE THIBAUT-POMERANTZ

Flammarion

ACKNOWLEDGMENTS

I would like to express my gratitude to the people who supported me throughout the creation of this book.

Firstly, the members of the public institutions who allowed me access to their collections and took the time to share with me their expertise : Dr Sabine Thümmler, curator of the Deutsches Tapetenmuseum in Kassel; Mme Véronique de La Hougue, curator of the Département des Papiers Peints at the Musée des Arts Décoratifs in Paris; Mme Dominique Deangeli-Cayol, archivist at the Bibliothèque Forney in Paris; M. Bernard Jacqué, curator of the Musée du Papier Peint in Rixheim; M. Philippe de Fabry, archivist at the Musée du Papier Peint in Rixheim; Mr. Greg Herringshaw, curator of the Wallcovering Department at the Cooper-Hewitt National Design Museum, New York.
I would also like to thank my close friends, Marie, Colette, and Jean-Marie, and particularly Anne-Laure, for their objectivity and invaluable advice.
And finally, my greatest thanks go to my husband, Alain Chastagnol who, with his erudition, his cultured spirit, and his aesthetic sensibility, but most of all through his persistent efforts to encourage—and even to provoke—me in my work, has led me to improve upon and open new doors onto my specialty, the art of wallpaper.

Translated from the French by Deke Dusinberre and Carolle Thibaut-Pomerantz

DESIGN
Bernard Lagacé

COPYEDITING
Andrea Belloli

PROOFREADING
Helen Woodhall

TYPESETTING
Anne-Lou Bissières

COLOR SEPARATION
Reproscan, Orio al Serio

Printed in Singapore by Tien Wah Press
Distributed in North America by Rizzoli
International Publications, Inc.

Simultaneously published in French as
Papiers Peints: Inspirations et Tendances
© Flammarion, Paris, 2009

English-language edition
© Flammarion, Paris, 2009

09 10 11 3 2 1
ISBN-13: 978-2-08-030109-3
Dépôt légal: 09/2009

COVER Imitation-silk *domino* with blue flowers and acanthus leaves, by Martin Bujon, Paris, c. 1760-70.
BACK COVER *Charmilles*, designed by Palyart in 1924 for the Maîtrise, Atelier d'Art of the Galeries Lafayette.
FOLD-UP FLAP *Lucullus*, printed in sepia and grisaille. This large frieze ran above the panel of *L'Automne* on Jules Desfossé's stand at the Exposition Universelle held in Paris in 1855.
INSIDE JACKET Large panel from the scenic wallpaper *Les Incas*, showing Pizarro's arrival in Peru, designed by Jean-François Marmontel, printed by Joseph Dufour, 1818.
PAGE 1 *Les Orties blanches*, wallpaper created for Atelier Martine, published by Paul Poiret, toward 1912. Bibliothèque Forney, Paris .
PAGE 2 Three-color *domino* with modern-seeming design, Augsburg, c. 1778. Musée des Arts Décoratifs, Paris.

10

32

132

84

CONTENTS

152

206

INTRODUCTION

My adventure with wallpaper began with a shock in Paris in 1986. I had wandered by chance into a room of the Drouot auction house; its walls were covered with an extraordinary profusion of wallpapers. It felt like Ali Baba's cave. I was dazzled and seduced by the variety of decors and the wealth of colors and I wanted to know more. I returned the next day and sat in the front row of the sales room, in order to have a better view of the wonderful papers unrolled by the auctioneer's assistants. Too tempting to resist, I made several purchases. My initiation took place under the enthusiastic guidance of Bernard Poteau, expert of that sale. A new world gradually found its way into my career, becoming a passion and a specialty that I have ardently promoted for over twenty years. After the initial aesthetic shock, I soon realized that, apart from by a few specialists and art connoisseurs, old wallpapers were relatively unknown. And *that* was the beginning of my *true* adventure—devoted to raising the public's awareness of this unique, forgotten art form. Believing deeply in their value, I have exhibited these wallpapers at all the prestigious art and antiques shows: the Biennale des Antiquaires in Paris, the European Fine Art Fair (TEFAF) in Maastricht, the Winter Antiques Show in New York, among others. I am still amazed by their power of attraction, as well as by the curiosity and questions they always provoke.

CHARACTERISTICS OF WALLPAPERS: DURABILITY AND ADAPTABILITY

Paper, invented by the early civilizations of the Middle East, Egypt, and China, is indeed the support used to create these mural coverings. Wallpapers, however, were not brush-painted, as in China, which probably led to the misleading French term *"papier peint"* (painted paper). In fact, craftsmen used wood-blocks to print European papers, called *"Tapete"* (wallcovering) in German and "wallpaper" in English.

These old papers are not fragile. The quality of the paper as well as that of the natural pigments have enabled them to survive poor atmospheric conditions, exposure to light and dust, and removal from one site to another. Some, but not all, can be salvaged and restored, but not by just anyone; such work calls for a specialized restorer.

Through ignorance or indifference, people have sometimes painted over period papers, destroying them irrevocably. Others have been glued directly onto plaster, making them very difficult to remove. And sometimes, when several layers of paper have been laid on top of one another, the restorer is like an archaeologist moving progressively back in time as layer after layer of rare and precious paper is uncovered.

The decision to restore wallpaper is usually made on the basis of its quality and rarity, assuming that it has substantially retained its original pigments and design and has not been excessively repainted. If done intelligently and with restraint, restoration will not diminish the value of a paper, but will, on the contrary, become part of its life cycle, providing a second life for centuries to come. Wallpaper is not an ephemeral art.

The main asset and particularity of wallpaper is its modular nature. It can be removed from a wall to be installed elsewhere or sold, as long as a paper conservator, who will do everything necessary to best preserve it, carries out this process. Thus these papers can be either rehung or mounted on canvas and stretchers like a painting.

Carolle Thibaut-Pomerantz in front of the floral decor by Henri Stephany, 1929–30. Kergorlay Collection, Paris.

PROVENANCE AND ATTRIBUTION OF WALLPAPERS

All the wallpapers I exhibit are period papers. The ones that have never been used are in perfect condition because they have remained rolled for a century or more. They generally come from the old stocks of former manufacturers or decorating firms. Some have been found in attics, the remnants of bygone purchases. As for papers that have already served their time on walls, the patina of age gives them added charm.

The provenance of a wallpaper is important. It is easy to establish if a paper is found in situ, where it was first hung, or has remained the property of one owner. Obviously, it is more difficult if a wallpaper has traveled and changed hands over the years. Furthermore, given the loss or destruction of many factory archives and sales ledgers, it can be problematic sometimes to establish the precise name and date of manufacture.

When it comes to attributions, manufacturers in the past often employed their own artists—designers and engravers—who usually remained anonymous, in order to preserve production secrets. There were a few exceptions, however: Réveillon hired well-known ornamental artists of his day; Dufour believed that it was useful to reveal the participation of certain artists and Zuber lured experienced art directors to his firm. Jules Desfossé, considered the finest manufacturer of the Second Empire (1850–70), was the first with the artist Thomas Couture, to sign their work, the famous *Les Prodigues* (The Prodigals) or *Souper de Pierrot* (Pierrot's Supper).

If it is difficult to ascertain the exact number of copies printed, one thing we do know is that the elaborate papers of the eighteenth and nineteenth centuries took a long time to produce. In the case of nineteenth-century scenic *panoramiques*, a complete set required several thousand wood-blocks and printing could last for over a year. Conceived as prestigious products that would establish a firm's image and fame, these decors were printed in very limited editions, generally between a hundred and a hundred and fifty, and sometimes only to order.

THE VALUE OF WALLPAPER AND ITS MARKET

The value of a period paper resides in the quality of unique skills involved in its production as well as its rarity. Wallpaper will be all the more valuable if it was printed in a limited edition over a limited period of time. If a decor was subsequently re-issued, it is preferable to seek out the original edition; older editions are more valuable, because as time passed, it became increasingly difficult to reproduce the fine engraving, subtle colors and shadings, quality of natural pigments, and the textures of these old papers. It is the combination of these elements that gives vintage wallpapers their incomparable character, imbuing them with a substance and presence that cannot be found in modern reproductions, even those supposedly made in the "traditional" manner. It is like comparing a piece of period furniture with a modern reproduction. For the past few years, period wallpapers have found their place on the art market. Their value continues to rise as examples become more and more rare. Thus vintage wallpapers have found their niche on the art market, following the trends and demand.

The value of these papers is reinforced by their presence in the collections of major museums across the world, by the many exhibitions and publications devoted to the subject, and by specialized auctions. Many have been preempted or designated as national treasures by the French state and other foreign governments, confirming that this art form is indeed considered part of a national heritage. Today, in a desire to broaden or complete their collections, museums in France and abroad continue to acquire both historic papers and those created by contemporary artists and designers.

Despite their rarity, it is still possible to discover beautiful period papers, and the idea of coming across a lost, hidden treasure is what motivates the passion of a true collector.

A WORLD TO REDISCOVER

As the object of a thriving trade, wallpapers moved around the globe. Some French papers were disseminated in the course of Napoleon's conquests, others were ordered by European courts and aristocracies; the wealthy or patrician families of the young American nation acquired many as well. Therefore, the most fascinating source for wallpapers is above all old fine houses, still standing throughout the world, that continue to harbor them. It is, in fact, the thrill of rediscovery that has led me on many exciting adventures, two of which are worth recounting. A few years ago, auctioneers in Caen, France, asked me to be an expert in a sale of eighteenth-century Chinese wallpapers. Thus I discovered Château Latour, once inhabited by Madame de Seran, a friend of Louis XV, by then no more than an empty shell exposed to the elements. Wandering through rooms where some of the most famous writers of the time had assembled, I discovered, like ghosts from the past, two superb eighteenth-century decors in the *Chambre aux Oiseaux* (Bird Bedroom) and the *Chambre aux Chinois* (Chinese Bedroom). Due to the accumulation of rubble between them and the walls on which they were tacked, the papers were in immediate danger of bursting and ripping. It was clear that they would not survive another winter and had to be rescued, without fail. Under difficult conditions, these splendid papers were successfully removed and restored, resurrected for another few centuries.

The other adventure occurred in the United States. I was contacted by some people whose dining room had suffered serious water damage; they were not interested in restoring the wallpaper installed by their parents. Looking at the photographs they supplied, I had a feeling that the papers were eighteenth-century and French. On my initiative and at my own risk, I had them removed, salvaging them in small pieces—a large puzzle to be reassembled afterwards. The restoration work turned out to be long and costly, but the reward was great: I found myself in possession of a rare decor, *Allégorie des Arts,* made between 1797 and 1801 by the famous architects Percier and Fontaine. Their original design is in the collection of the Musée des Arts Décoratifs in Paris. Furthermore, this particular set came from the Lasker residence in Lake Forest, near Chicago, Illinois, built by the architect David Adler and decorated by Frances Elkins in the 1920s.

I sincerely hope that through this book, I can, in turn open a door onto a most magical world and enable readers to discover a unique area of the decorative arts. Wallpaper has been constantly renewed throughout the years. Today it is a growing field, attracting numerous artists and designers who are fascinated by its rich motifs and bold colors.

Wallpaper is capable of reflecting fashion in all its modes. Essentially a trendsetter, it has become a mural art form in its own right, brilliantly revealing the history, evolution of tastes, and aspirations of each successive epoch. It is hardly surprising then, that since its beginnings up to the present day, wallpaper has never ceased to be in vogue.

CAROLLE THIBAUT-POMERANTZ

THE ORIGINS
OF WALLPAPER

The use of paper as a decorative wall covering began as early as the sixteenth century. Its origins go back to two inventions, namely those of paper and printing. Westerners, who first learned of them through the publication of Marco Polo's *Travels* in 1298, rediscovered them later, initially in the form of wood-block prints first made in the Netherlands in 1418. Thus from the beginning, printing designs on paper derived from the art of engraving, and only briefly predated the printed text, which was made possible by Johannes Gutenberg's crucial invention of movable type around 1450. Printers, identifying themselves with signs such as *Le Soleil d'Or* (The Golden Sun), *Le Soufflet Vert* (The Green Bellows), and *L'Homme Sauvage* (The Wild Man), soon flourished in the Latin Quarter in Paris, as well as in other major cities in France, notably Lyons. Texts and illuminations were printed to illustrate books of hours, almanacs, and chivalric romances, as well as tales of New World exploration, in particular of New Guinea by the Portuguese in 1450, of America by Christopher Columbus in 1492, followed by Vasco de Gama's circumnavigation of the Cape of Good Hope in 1497.

Thus the technique of making decorative papers was closely linked not only to the development of printing but also to the spirit of exploration.

During this period, France was manufacturing *domino* papers, a name perhaps of Italian origin, known to be in use in 1401. *Dominos* were small sheets, roughly 20 by 14 inches (50 by 36 centimeters), composed of identical repeat motifs printed from an engraved block of wood, often pear wood. The first *dominos* were printed in black with a single block, while more elaborate ones were created with several blocks and then colored with a brush or stencil in red, blue, brown, yellow, purple, and green. Initially, the designs of these papers were stylistically rather simple and a slightly crude.

Domino makers were craftsmen working in paper and cardboard, printing and painting decorative sheets with pictures of religious subjects, as well as playing cards. Over time, these small sheets became more varied adding stripes, checks, and mosaics, and they were used as

Imitation-silk domino (single-sheet paper) with blue flowers and acanthus leaves, by Martin Bujon, Paris, c. 1760-70. Carolle Thibaut-Pomerantz Collection.

lining papers for bookbindings, boxes, chests, and cupboards, as well as for fire screen coverings and other paneled surfaces.

By the sixteenth century, business had expanded to such a degree that craftsmen were obliged to organize into guilds—Louis XI granted them their own special banner. The guild of "card makers, master *domino* printers, and picture-print makers" was founded in 1540.

During the Renaissance, castles in France no longer played a military role. At the same time, the frequent marriages of French princes to rich Italian heiresses created a new lifestyle in which luxury was inspired by ancient Rome, especially Nero's palatial Domus Aurea, whose walls were decorated with delicate foliate scrolls and grotesques. Gradually, a society of nouveaux riches—affluent merchants, financiers, and other burghers—developed. They could not afford, however, to furnish their homes with such costly decorative items as the luxurious Flemish tapestries, precious marbles, grand leather from Cordoba, and rich fabrics and velvets from Genoa. They therefore turned to the imitation products made by "card and *domino* makers." These wallpapers were first used in fine boutiques and small manor houses; then, encouraged by the spreading fashion, papermakers began producing more complex, yet less costly, products which attracted a wider clientele.

In 1597, Henry IV issued a decree recognizing "the makers of painted and printed papers for lining walls and other uses." Many *domino* workshops sprang up not only in Paris but also in Orléans, Chartres, Le Mans, Rouen, Troyes, and elsewhere in France, as well as in Italy where the Remondini printing dynasty developed in Bassano.

Domino makers were soon covering walls with patterns of joined papers, *papiers raboutés*, a technique that was established around 1690, as described by Jacques Savary des Bruslons in his *Dictionnaire Universel du Commerce* (Universal Dictionary of Trade, 1723–30). The mastery of the joined paper process swiftly transformed the printing trade, permitting much greater freedom for a decor in continuity: *tableau tenture* (wallcovering) or architectural ensemble. Many print shops converted to the production of such wallpapers.

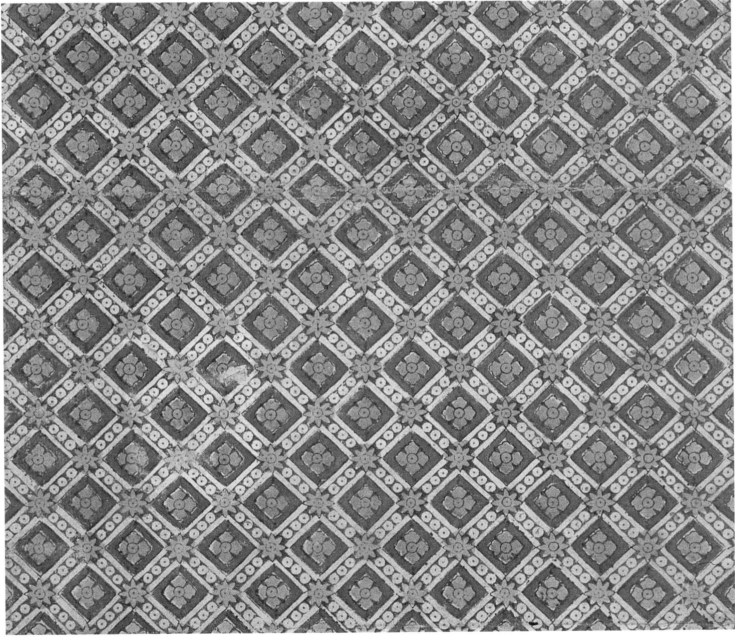

TOP *B*ox covered with a *domino* paper, Sevestre Le Blond workshop, Orléans,
mid-18th century. Musée des Arts Décoratifs, Paris (formerly Pierre Deux Collection, New York).

ABOVE, LEFT *D*ecorative paper with floral garland against a blue-and-white grid. Ducal Palace,
the manufacturer Remondini, Bassano, late 18th–early 19th century. Deutsches Tapetenmuseum, Kassel.

ABOVE, RIGHT *F*ragment of paper wall hanging with fleurs-de-lis motif, from the Château de Marcoux,
second half of the 17th century. Musée des Arts Décoratifs, Paris.

FACING PAGE *W*allpaper with bird and poppy design, by the manufacturer Fourcroy, Paris, c. 1700.
Musée des Arts Décoratifs, Paris.

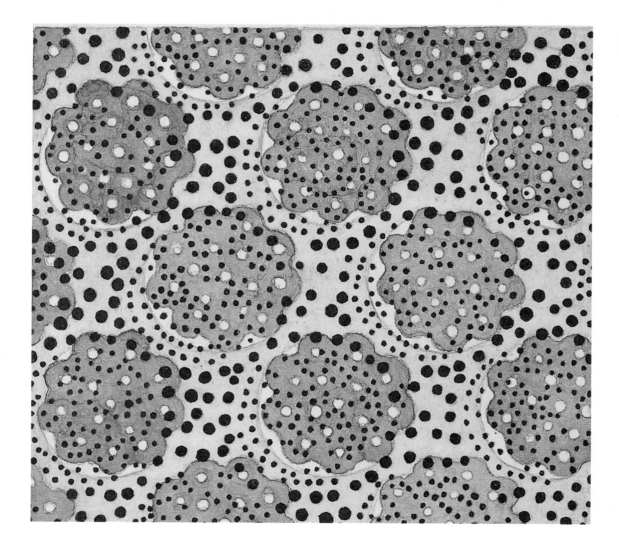

RIGHT *Three-color domino*, Augsburg, c. 1778 (very modern design). Musée des Arts Décoratifs, Paris.

FACING PAGE *Domino* with flower-and-ribbon pattern, similar to block-printed and stenciled papers of Orléans workshops distributed collectively through *À Paris chez les Associés*, c. 1770. Carolle Thibaut-Pomerantz Collection.

1. Henri Clouzot and Charles Follot, *Histoire du papier peint en France du XVIIe au XIXe siècle* (Paris: Éditions d'Art Charles Moreau, 1935), pp. 15–16. This book is the earliest and most important reference work on the subject. Clouzot was curator at the Bibliothèque Forney in Paris from 1908 to 1920, and director and curator of the Musée Galliera (Musée des Arts Décoratifs de la Ville de Paris) from 1920 to 1935.
2. Pierre Gusman, *Panneaux décoratifs et tentures murales du XVIIIe siècle et du commencement du XIXe siècle* (Paris: Charles Massin, 1900), p. 2; trans. by Geert Wisse as "Manifold Beginnings: Single-Sheet Papers," in Lesley Hoskins (ed.), *The Papered Wall* (New York: Harry N. Abrams, 1994), p. 14.

In Paris, the Papillon workshop (a great dynasty of engravers founded by Jean Papillon I, wood-block engraver and master *domino* maker), which had moved to rue Saint-Jacques in the Latin Quarter around 1662, marked the history of wallpaper. Around 1688, one of the most skilled woodcutters, Jean Papillon II, invented the printing technique to produce *papier de tapisserie* (tapestry paper). His descendant, Jean-Baptiste-Michel Papillon, described this advance in a practical treatise on woodcut techniques: "We owe to [Jean II] the invention in Paris of *papiers de tapisserie* which he brought into fashion in the year 1688. He knew how to hang them with good taste, much art, and meticulous care. He took this invention to greater heights than ever before."[1]

In France, the development and vogue for *papier de tapisserie* were encouraged by the 1686 ban on the manufacture and importation of calico, the fashionable printed cotton fabrics brought back from India by Dutch missionaries and widely imitated by workshops in Holland, Germany, and Flanders. *Papier de tapisserie*—conceived in the same spirit with squares intermingling flowers, fruit, animals, and grotesques—replaced these large cotton wallcoverings.

This type of tapestry-like paper . . . had long been used only by country folk and the more modest classes in Paris . . . [but] was raised to such a peak of perfection and attractiveness that . . . there was not a house in Paris, however magnificent, that did not have somewhere, be it in a dressing room or an even more secret area, that was not covered and pleasantly adorned with such material.[2]

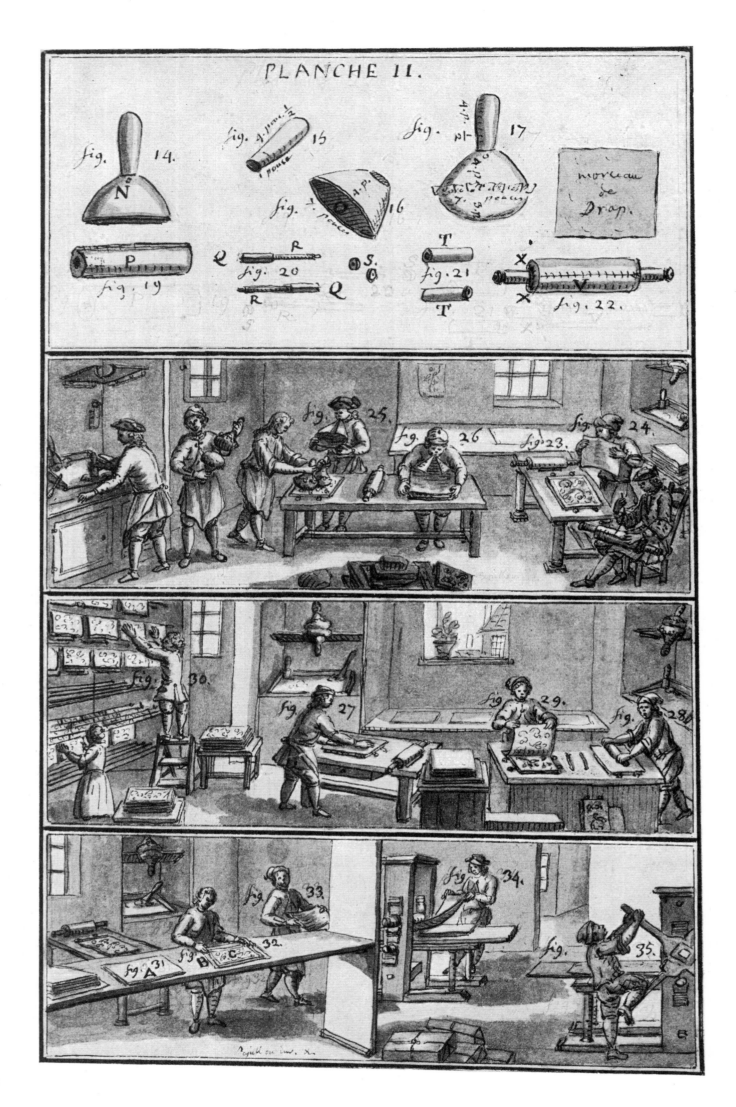

FACING PAGE *One* of seven plates produced by Jean-Michel Papillon to illustrate the entry on *dominoterie* (decorative papers) for Diderot's *Encylopédie* (1751–52), but not included in the final publication. These plates, extremely important for the history of wallpaper, were first published in 1925 by Gusman and later by Clouzot. Cabinet des Estampes, Bibliothèque Nationale de France, Paris.

ABOVE, TOP *Two*-color wallpaper imitating lace, printed in England, late 17th century. Victoria and Albert Museum, London.

ABOVE, BOTTOM *Fragment* of tapestry-like wallpaper, specialty of Atelier Papillon, wood-block printed architectural decor and hand-painted, 1723–40. Musée des Art Décoratifs, Paris.

ABOVE *Fragment* of tapestry-like wallpaper from the Gottrau manor in Léchelles, Fribourg, Switzerland, 18th century. Musée du Papier Peint, Rixheim.

The desire to perfect the imitation of material itself favored the fashion for what became known as "flock papers." Around 1620, a paper- and sheath maker from Rouen named Le François devised a method of adding colored wool fibers to areas where a mordant had been applied, thus creating the illusion of a velvety surface. The English nevertheless maintain that the application of this innovation to paper dates to 1634 and should be credited to Jeremy Lanyer, a Frenchman then living in England. They had also developed an early craft of wallpaper, the oldest specimen being the "Cambridge fragment" made in 1509 by Hugo Goes, an engraver and printer from York. Discovered in Christ Church, Cambridge, it imitated the brocaded fabrics highly appreciated in Europe at that time.

The origins and techniques of English wallpaper can also be traced back to leather makers in an era when embossed, gilt leather was a highly prized wall covering. In London, the first workshops were located in the neighborhood of Saint Paul's Cathedral, the best-known leather gilders being Hall, Bromwich, and Crompton & Spinnage who also made imitation leather. By the mid-eighteenth century, interest in leather gave way to the growing appeal of wallpaper. The famous Blue Paper Warehouse in Aldermanbury, founded in 1702, perfected the art of flock papers, also known as "blue papers." Relatively simple at first, by 1730 their baroque designs were being enhanced with large branch motifs that imitated damask and velvet fabrics. These more refined papers replaced tapestries, silks, and velvets at much less cost. Such "English papers" enjoyed their heyday around 1750, when they were extensively exported across Europe.

The vogue for flock papers swept through the formal homes of well-to-do Englishmen. A few of these interiors remain intact today, such as Christ Church Mansion in Ipswich, Suffolk, and Clandon Park in Surrey. Flock paper also graced the Privy Council Chamber in London's Whitehall, the Queen's drawing room in Hampton Court Palace, and the Portsmouth, New Hampshire home of the American colony's last royal governor, John Wentworth.

Around the mid-eighteenth century, the English, imitating the Chinese, developed a distemper printing technique: water-based pigments were applied to a paper hand-brushed in color producing a sharper design and rich, mat shades, which became one of wallpaper's foremost characteristics. Since Papillon had already experimented with this technique, with less success, the French continued to print with ink and oil.

During the same period, the English also perfected the technique of joined sheets of paper glued together, prior to printing, to obtain rolls measuring 9 ells (12 yards or 11 meters) long. It took twenty-four sheets to make one roll. This method offered greater freedom in producing continuous patterns on a larger scale.

Therefore, around 1765, thanks to these two major technical advances, wallpaper entered a new era, becoming a genuine mural art form.

Throughout the 1700s, technical progress combined with the improved quality of life of the affluent English that encouraged their desire for novelty and originality to transform this craft into a veritable industry. The pace of production accelerated. Homes became more comfortable, and wallpaper became an important feature of interior decoration. Thus every town and country house soon had at least one important room whose walls were adorned with wallpaper.

The manufacturers—known as "paperhanging makers" or "paper stainers"—also became interior-design consultants, setting the tone for wealthy, fashion-hungry London society.

RIGHT *G*reen salon of Clandon Park, example of a foliage flock wallpaper, c. 1735. Very fashionable at the time, such papers were used at Clandon Park, Surrey, His Majesty's Privy Council in London, and at Hampton Court.

FACING PAGE *D*etail of a blue flock paper with large baroque leaves, c. 1735, similar to those hung in Clandon Park, Surrey and Christchurch Mansion, Ipswich. Victoria and Albert Museum, London.

They became true trendsetters. Amongst the best known was Thomas Bromwich, whose Ludgate Hill company ("Paperhanging, Manufacturers to Her Majesty," 1670–1853) specialized in papier-mâché which imitated plaster moldings and stuccowork, and provided substitutes for interior architectural ornamentation. Meanwhile, Eckhart Brothers on Old Bond Street and the famous interior decorators Crace & Sons enjoyed the patronage of George III.[3] The English also introduced "mock papers" (or "India papers"); known as "chintz", whose small flowers imitated Indian cotton prints.

The celebrated John Baptist Jackson of Battersea also tried to bring innovations to the art of English wallpaper. He first went to Paris in 1726 to study woodcut engraving with either Jean-Baptiste-Michel Papillon or Vincent Le Sueur. He then traveled to Italy where he found his inspiration, producing papers of an Italianate style with chiaroscuro effects and baroque borders. None of his work remains in situ, but some preparatory designs have been preserved in the Victoria and Albert Museum in London.

Jackson is also linked to the concept of print rooms in which engravings were applied directly to the wall and framed with a border of wallpaper. This fashion was launched by Lord Cadogan in 1750 and applied by Horace Walpole, a fine amateur and connoisseur of wallpapers, in his home, Strawberry Hill. The finest existing example in situ is Woodhall Park in Hertfordshire. This fashion led to the creation of the typically English "print-room papers" on blue or yellow ground that imitated the look and feeling of an English collection of prints hung on the wall.

Other English papers that were fashionable at the time ranged from Oriental-inspired rococo patterns to the classicism of the Adam brothers, with a distinct preference for the Gothic style, which combined naturalistic floral decor with ornamental architectural elements, such as the favorite "pillar and arch" motif.

The English industry thus dominated the European and American markets up to the middle of the eighteenth century when cross-channel competition increased, exacerbating the commercial rivalry that had existed between France and England since the Seven Years' War (1756–63). A veritable "paper war" was declared.

Importation of English papers clearly introduced English taste to the French, which by the end of the eighteenth century extended to other realms such as gardening and fashion accessories. In 1753 the French ambassador to England, the duc de Mirepoix, brought flock papers back to Paris, while Lord Albemarle, the English ambassador to France, imported them to decorate his home in Passy. The memoirs of the novelist Madame de Genlis attest to this fashion: "Magnificent Gobelins tapestries are being consigned to dressing rooms, to be replaced by English blue-paper."[4]

Under the influence of Madame de Pompadour, "the queen of good taste," these papers even reached France's royal residences. In 1754 she used them to decorate the walls of her dressing room and the hallway leading to her chapel in Versailles, and in 1758 she adorned the walls of her bathroom at the Château de Champs.

Starting in 1760, prompted by these imports, French workshops—notably Papillon and Didier Aubert in Charenton—outdid themselves to produce more refined and less expensive flock papers. Countless advertisements proclaimed the superiority, quality, and elegance of Parisian flock papers, thus encouraging the fashion for overall, aligned patterns. Good patriot that she was, Mademoiselle d'Henery, owner of a workshop on rue de la Comtesse-d'Artois, stated in the *Mercure de France* in 1774 that "the excellence [of French flock papers] comes from the fact that only French designs are used, and they are endowed with all the grace

3. The wallpaper manufacturers Crace & Sons was founded in 1768 by Edward Crace, the first in a long line of English decorators. Frederick Crace (1779–1859) would decorate Windsor Palace and the Brighton Pavilion (1817–23) with fine examples of Chinoiserie, while John Gregory Crace (1809–1889), the last of the line, was a historian of wallpaper who published *The History of Paper Hanging* (1889).
4. See Françoise Teynac, Pierre Nolot, and Jean-Denis Vivien, *Le Monde du papier peint* (Paris: Berger-Levrault, 1981), p. 71.

ABOVE An example of the print-room decoration made fashionable by Lord Cadogan, c. 1750. Castletown House, County Kildare, Ireland.

FACING PAGE Detail of a yellow-ground "print room" paper from Doddington Hall, Lincolnshire, c. 1760. Victoria and Albert Museum, London.

27

ABOVE *I*nterior of a house decorated with famous "pillar and arch" wallpaper.
Oil painting attributed to Srickland Lowny, c. 1760. National Gallery of Ireland, Dublin.

FACING PAGE *E*xample of blue "pillar and arch" paper on a yellow ground from the Old Manor,
Bourton-on-the-Water, Gloucestershire, c. 1769. Victoria and Albert Museum, London.

and elegance typical of all French workmanship." Among the most popular patterns were roses, bouquets, ribbons, imitation fabrics, and Chinese motifs.

France soon surpassed its neighbors in terms of technical mastery and refinement. English production, in contrast, went into decline, hampered by taxes on printed, painted, and hung papers, and by the cost of licenses, which were carefully controlled by the Excise Office from 1712 to 1835. In order to protect itself from European—especially French—competition, all imports of wallpaper into England were banned in 1773. Its borders would not be reopened until 1861.

The French king, meanwhile, decreed protective measures for French flock papers in 1766, thus encouraging their technical and decorative progress. The monarch levied a tax of 20 livres per hundredweight on imports, whereas exported French flock papers were taxed only 20 sous. French wallpaper thus not only permanently dethroned *domino* papers, but English production as well. Even the English recognized that their more affordable papers could no longer compete with the wonderful French wallpapers, which were superior in quality, elegance, and originality.

RIGHT *R*ed flock paper on a gray ground, France, late 18th century. Bibliothèque Forney, Paris.

ABOVE *D*amask design in red flock paper, Jean-Baptiste Réveillon
c. 1770. Deutsches Tapetenmuseum, Kassel
(former Bernard Poteau Collection).

LEFT *L*arge damask design in yellow flock paper, Jean-Baptiste Réveillon,
c. 1770. Bibliothèque Forney, Paris.

THE TRIUMPH OF ORNAMENTAL DESIGNERS

In the eighteenth century, France—then Europe's most populous country, with twenty-two million inhabitants—set the standards in both the fine and the decorative arts. Stimulated by the wealth of royal and aristocratic luxury, France's growing influence provided the impetus for artistic creation. French wallpaper reached a level of refinement that would spread throughout the world. The ornamental designers, inspired by the works of artists and fashions of the day—a vogue for exoticism, an infatuation with flowers, and a return to Antiquity— contributed immeasurably to its impact.

Trade with the East encouraged the penchant for exoticism, more specifically for *Chinoiserie*. As in the field of important discoveries made by explorers and missionaries, three countries were involved in a long, fierce competition for the monopoly on this lucrative trade in spices and extraordinary luxury items: England, who was the first, created the British East India Company in 1599; Holland, in 1602, set up the Vereenigde Oost-Indische Compagnie; and France, in 1664, established the Compagnie des Indes Orientales (founded by Louis XIV's chief minister, Colbert). Following a ban on imports of Indian calico in 1688, the French sought to bring down the Dutch company and take over its profitable trade. Within a short space of time London and Paris became the two major centers of distribution.

The merchandise that so inspired European decorative arts came from India, China, and Japan. For example, the famous calico prints—cotton fabrics painted by hand or block-printed, known as "chintz" in English—had arrived in the West by the early seventeenth century, leading to the establishment in 1648 of the first French firm in Marseilles. Embossed and gilded papers from Japan , both lavish and sturdy, as well as porcelain, lacquer ware, silk, and wallpaper from China were also imported. Chinese wallpapers, discovered by Dutch missionaries in the sixteenth century, were deemed too fragile to travel, so at first only sea captains brought

Stylized leaf and flower pattern on ground flocked by powdered wool in shades of crimson, the manufacturer Réveillon, c. 1770. Musée des Arts Décoratifs, Paris.

ABOVE AND FACING PAGE *H*and-painted Chinese wallpaper decorated with delicate white birds and flowers on a green ground, 18th century. Château Mouton-Rothschild Collection, Pauillac, France.

PAGES 36-37 *H*and-painted Chinese wallpaper with large birds in fruit- and flower-laden trees on an ecru ground, originally from the Chambre aux Oiseaux, Château Latour, Normandy, 18th century. Private collection.

them back to Europe as personal gifts. These papers, hand-painted in gouache and highlighted in ink, could explain the origin of the specific French term "*papier peint*". Their patterns, devoid of shading, contrasted sharply with the ecru background of rice paper, which sometimes was colored or gilded.

Oblivious to the rules of perspective so cherished by the Renaissance, the imagery on these papers presented no illusion of depth and was to be viewed in a continuous, panoramic sweep. They depicted birds, flowers, the tree of life, landscapes, and everyday scenes, all typical Chinese subjects. Delivered in the form of large sheets, these papers could in fact be transported easily, and be combined afterwards to create a full decor. Backed with canvas or jute and mounted on wooden frames, they could be nailed to the wall and removed easily if necessary.

Extensively imported by the English starting in the eighteenth century, these papers were then imitated, and even executed by craftsmen who were brought from China in order to better satisfy the tastes of the local market. Counterfeit copies of these wallpapers were produced in Flanders, Holland, and, above all, Germany, using an oilcloth base to suggest the precious texture of lacquer. European demand prompted the Chinese to begin producing the papers in series from copperplate engravings, hand-colored with a brush or stencil. But the original eighteenth-century papers remain the most refined and most rare.

In England, the popularity of these papers was such that every member of eighteenth-century high society had a "Chinese room" in his home. The splendid wallpapers given to Lord Macartney at the end of the eighteenth century during his embassy to Peking can still be seen in the Coutts Bank in London. These fine papers would remain in fashion into the following century, as evidenced by the large *salon* at Carlton House in London, at Windsor Castle, and at Brighton Pavilion.

In France, the rage for exoticism and *Chinoiserie* soared in 1670, when Louis XIV, totally enamored with Madame de Montespan, offered her a "Porcelain Trianon" in blue-and-white faïence "done in the manner of objects from China," which the Dutch in Delft were imitating so extensively. In the 1750s, François Boucher applied Chinese imagery on the walls of the Château de Belleville, to the delight of Madame de Pompadour, and used the same motifs in the cartoons for his well-known tapestries. Boucher also adorned his theater decors with festive and romantic Chinese and Indian scenes.

Jean Aubert and Blaise Nicolas Le Sueur decorated Frederick the Great's Chinese pavilion at his palace Sanssouci in Potsdam. Christophe Huet excelled in composing scenes of Tartars, Chinese figures, monkeys, and pastoral landscapes in monochrome shades of blue, as can still be seen at the Hôtel Matignon in Paris.

Every aristocratic residence had its "Chinese study" with porcelains mounted in gilt-bronze as well as Louis XV commodes decorated with Chinese lacquer, introducing a touch of exoticism into the interiors. Chinese wallpapers remained the height of decorative fashion from 1740 to 1790.

China was not the sole source of exoticism, however. As early as in 1686, Louis XIV received the Embassy of the King of Siam on a golden Persian carpet. Then amid the glitter of the Hall of Mirrors, he welcomed the special ambassador from Persia as depicted in a magnificent painting by Antoine Coypel. Later, in 1720 and 1740, Louis XV received two special envoys from the Ottoman Sultan. Infatuation with all things Turkish was such that no fashionable home could be without its allusion to the Levant, as is illustrated in Jean-Baptiste Vanmour's 1712 album of prints, *Recueil de Cent Estampes*. Turkish ornament was reflected in dress, (the livery of black servants), paintings (Laurent de la Hyre's colorful fancies), literature (Montesquieu's *Persian Letters*), opera–ballet (Rameau's *Indes Galantes* in 1735), later, in the music of Mozart, and, of course, in wallpapers.

This mixture of exoticism inspired one to dream, and offered a welcome counter-balance imposed by the formal Academicism of Charles Lebrun on the "Apollonian" art of the Sun King, Louis XIV. Flowers—already a favorite motif of *domino* papers—and sinuous curves triumphed over other motifs and soon rejuvenated the baroque and rococo styles popular under of Louis XV. Ornamental designers in France—inspired by the likes of Claude Gillot, Antoine Watteau, François Boucher, Carle van Loo, Jean Bérain, Claude Audran III, and Jean-Baptiste Oudry—would exploit flowers in all their forms: bouquets, festoons, vases, and baskets. Garlands of roses and wildflowers hung from the necks of putti and the ribbons of shepherds.

Jean-Baptiste Pillement (1727–1808) occupied a special place among these ornamentalists. Having begun his career as a designer of tapestries for the Gobelins Manufactory in Paris

40

FACING PAGE "Chinese-style" wallpaper with a corn-motif border, block-printed by a Berlin factory, 1797. Residence of Frederick-William III and Louise of Prussia, Schloss Paretz Collection, Potsdam.

ABOVE Hand-painted Chinese wallpaper on a yellow ground, c. 1800. Bedroom of Queen Victoria, Royal Pavilion, Brighton.

ABOVE "Chinese-style" English wallpaper, wood-block printed by Eckhardt Bros, c. 1769. Victoria and Albert Museum, London.

FACING PAGE "Chinese-style" wallpaper on a red ground, wood-block printed by the manufacturer Réveillon, Paris, 1771. Musée du Papier Peint, Rixheim (formerly Follot Collection).

and of silk fabrics for a major workshop in Lyons, he traveled across Europe, living for many years in England before ending his career in France. In 1778 he became court painter to Marie-Antoinette, assigned to redecorate the Petit Trianon with a profusion of flowers. Pillement contributed enormously to the interest in *Chinoiserie* in both England and France. He was commissioned to create Chinese rooms, which ultimately became known as *Salons Pillement*. He was perhaps the most prolific and talented artist of this delightful rococo fantasy, producing over a forty-year period some thirteen hundred engraved designs—an inexhaustible resource for wallpaper manufacturers.

While his output reflected the taste of his day, Pillement also embodied a return to nature—as did Marie-Antoinette herself, who preferred the hermitage of the Petit Trianon with its rustic hamlet to the Château of Versailles with its Hall of Mirrors. This return to untamed nature was rediscovered by Jean-Jacques Rousseau and heralded in his novel *The New Heloise* (1761).

Flowers henceforth came to dominate decoration. The outdoors moved into the indoors: the garden introduced itself onto wood paneling, commodes, armchairs, beds, and curtains, covering every space in the house. The transformation into a more relaxed lifestyle led to more intimate spaces, with specific rooms all calling for the use of wallpaper whose bright colors brought youth and gaiety to mural decoration.

Joseph-Laurent Malaine, known as the "Flower Painter," worked for the French king at the Gobelins Manufactory in 1787, and was then hired as a designer, in turn, by the wallpaper workshops of Hartmann Risler, Réveillon, Jacquemart & Bénard, Arthur & Robert, and, finally, Dollfus (later partner to Zuber), where he became the art director. Malaine designed some of the finest floral wallpapers ever created.

Other inspirations came from voyages to Italy: the development of a neo-classical vocabulary and an interest in the poetic ruins so beautifully depicted in paintings by Hubert Robert and Jean-Honoré Fragonard. Similarly, Jean-Baptiste Huet popularized the grotesques and the *arabesques* found in The Raphael Loggia. After a trip to Italy in 1749, François de Marigny, Madame de Pompadour's brother and future director of the Royal Works, combined rococo decoration with Greek-key and linear motifs.

*I*mposing floral composition design by Joseph-Laurent Malaine, the "Flower Painter", emerging in front of a subtly evoked garden in the background. One panel of a pair, wood-block printed and attributed to Hartmann Risler & Co., Mulhouse, c. 1795. Musée des Arts Décoratifs, Paris (Zuber Donation, 1882).

The discovery of Pompeii and Herculaneum, as seen through the engravings published by Cochin and Bellicar in 1754, contributed greatly to the important upheaval in decoration. French artists passing through or residing in Rome were fascinated by the archaeological excavations and seduced by the elegance and refinement of the frescoes being brought to light. A new aesthetic vocabulary emerged. Lavallée-Poussin, in collaboration with the engraver Guyot, published a series of plates of interlacing ornament that he designed in Rome. By the end of the eighteenth century, a plethora of documents related to the *arabesques* found in the baths of Livia and Hadrian's villa could be found in works by Piranesi, Caylus (a famous collector and art patron), the archaeologist Winckelmann, and de Ponce. This infatuation for Antiquity and the revived Pompeian style perfectly suited wallpaper, which no longer sought to imitate fabrics and finally emerged as a mural art distinct from all others.

The supremacy of taste, technical mastery, and high-quality manufacturing combined to make France "the" leading country for wallpaper. Around 1780, French industry registered thirty thousand workers and thirty Parisian workshops, of which the best known were Legrand & Cie, and Arthur, an Englishman already established in 1772, who associated with Grenard in 1775, and in 1789 with Robert, to become Arthur & Robert.

However, the unrivaled master remained Jean-Baptiste Réveillon who began his career in 1741 as a stationer and notions merchant. In 1755, having been accepted first into the guild of copper-plate engravers and then into that of painters and sculptors, Réveillon set up a paper factory in the hamlet of Courtalin in Brie, while also opening a workshop for painted and printed wallpapers in the Faubourg Saint-Antoine district of Paris.

With the outbreak of the Seven Years' War in 1756, Réveillon faced the challenge of producing the famous flock papers so prized by the English. He would soon match—and then surpass—them in quality. He copied the English technique of printing distemper colors on vellum paper, and perfected the gluing of sheets into rolls. Showing remarkable mastery of these new methods, he produced larger, more elaborate and more durable wallpapers with richer materials, and more varied and delicate colors. One of his secrets was the skill of his three hundred employees, whom he organized into specialized workshops: paper gluers, color grinders, background-brushers, printers, engravers, designers, and painters.

Réveillon developed three distinct categories of wallpaper: a luxury collection requiring over ninety blocks (Madame de Genlis observed that such papers cost as much as silks and tapestries); so-called "common" papers (seven to eight blocks) for the average market; and ordinary papers using just a single color. He was the first wallpaper manufacturer to realize that his superiority resided in his choice of artists. He hired many textile designers, some even from the Gobelins Manufactory, commissioning them to recreate motifs taken from the most important painters. Many of his decors were inspired by the designs of ornamentalist-artists such as Cietti, Lavallée-Poussin, Huet, Prieur, and Boucher the Younger.

Réveillon also proved to be an unrivaled master of the *arabesque* decors, which he elaborated in multiple forms through many highly refined compositions. He remained so representative of this style that often high-quality *arabesques* are attributed to him to the detriment of other manufacturers.

Furthermore, he surpassed the competition thanks to his successful tactical battles against the guilds, his thorough knowledge of the profession, and his remarkable artistic taste. His obvious grasp of the flourishing market paved the way for extraordinary financial success.

Réveillon opened a shop on the Place du Carrousel, opposite the Tuileries Palace, and in 1783 obtained the title of "Royal Manufacturer." In 1786 he won an industrial award and a medal for his art in paperwork. His factory, La Folie-Titon, established in 1767, became a genuine palace-like manufacturer with a central garden worthy of a prince.

PAGE 52 *Grand Ananas* (Large Pineapple), India-style floral pattern of branches with floral and exotic fruit. Wood-block printed by Réveillon, 1789. Bibliothèque Forney, Paris.

PAGE 53 *India-style paper with colorful flowers, fruit, and birds on a vermiculated beige ground, wood-block printed by Jean-Baptiste Réveillon, Paris, 1786. Carolle Thibaut-Pomerantz Collection. A similar example is in the Musée du Papier Peint, Rixheim.

ABOVE AND FACING PAGE Suite of four *arabesque* panels. From left to right: Flora Distributing Flowers, Flora after Poussin, Bacchantes with Tambourine, Venus in a Chariot Pulled by Butterflies. These panels, in pristine condition and of remarkable freshness, consist of wood-block printed outlines, hand-painted colors in ink wash with figures highlighted in gold leaf. Jean-Baptiste Réveillon, Royal Manufacture, Paris, 1788 (design no. 600 conserved in the Musée des Arts Décoratifs, Paris). Carolle Thibaut-Pomerantz Collection (formerly Henri Samuel Collection). Identical papers are also in the public collections of the Musée des Arts Décoratifs, Paris; Musée du Papier Peint, Rixheim; and Cooper-Hewitt National Design Museum, New York.

Exporting his products throughout the world, Réveillon's fame spread far beyond the kingdom and gave this new form of decorative art its noble reputation. Henri Clouzot, the first historian of wallpaper, wrote that Réveillon "taught wallpaper to speak a new language."[1]

The fashion for exoticism, the appeal of floral decoration, the return to Antiquity, and the artistic talents of Réveillon were the four essential reasons for the triumph of masterpieces of French wallpaper. Yet there was still one further step before this offspring of fine engraving could be considered a full-fledged art: royal sanction.

When the French populace forced the king and queen to leave Versailles at the start of the Revolution in 1789, they returned to the Tuileries Palace that had not been lived in since 1722 and was in a wretched state. How could the stately setting required by ceremonial etiquette be re-established quickly? It was not only the urgency of the mission, but also the critical condition of government finances that prompted the Commissioner General of the Royal Household, Thierry de Ville-d'Avray, to turn to wallpaper, which could be acquired more quickly and less expensively than the silk weavings from Lyons. He therefore called upon the leading paper manufacturers, Arthur & Robert and Réveillon.

The dazzling effect of these papers lent new gaiety, grandeur, and nobility to the rooms of the Tuileries. They adorned the walls of the king's office and bedchamber, the queen's dining room, and the bedroom of their daughter, Madame Royale. The patterns featured *arabesques*, pilasters, medallions, and cameos in the "Etruscan manner," which made Arthur & Robert's papers so famous.

There were also monochrome panels edged with the floral garlands that had been made fashionable by the queen. These plain backgrounds, or *unis pour unis* (totally undecorated and plain), had to be faultless and were therefore costly; others, *unis pour impression* (plain grounds for later printing), were easier to manufacture.

The interior decoration of the Tuileries Palace and the vogue it inspired soon spread not only through France but also elsewhere in Europe and America. It was imitated in Italy in Civitavecchia and at Thun Palace in Vigo di Ton, in Trentino-Alto Adige; in Russia at Count Sheremetiev's Ostankino palace north of Moscow; in Germany at Schloss Favorite in Ludwigsburg, Schlossgut Schmidt in Guntersblum, Hesse, Pfaueninsel (Peacock Island) and Schloss Paretz near Berlin; in England at Moccas Court in Herefordshire; and in Sweden at Rydboholm Castle.[2]

These "French-style" wallpapers, chosen above all for convenience as well as the elegance of the decors that they provided, had an impact on the evolution of taste. They perhaps represent Marie-Antoinette's last contribution to the arts, which even the guillotine could not eradicate.

Indeed, the French Revolution halted neither the industry nor the inspiration behind wallpaper manufacture. One of its direct effects, however, was the "Réveillon affair": a group of workers in Paris, convinced that Réveillon was part of a plot against the working class, stormed his handsome factory on April 28, 1789, looting and burning it. Production did not begin again until the following autumn. At that point Réveillon began to withdraw from the business, first renting his factory to Jacquemart & Bénard and finally selling it to them in 1792.

Politics even affected manufacturers who were more sympathetic to the Revolution: Arthur, a Jacobin linked to Robespierre, was guillotined in 1799, as were Grenard and Cietti. Carrying on what had made Réveillon's success, Jacquemart & Bénard became one of the leading producers of the day.

Conforming to propaganda, wallpaper became a medium for new themes for the new centers of government or for the innumerable Revolutionary celebrations. An abundance of new designs appeared: allegories of the Nation, Law, and King, combining the royal

1. Henri Clouzot and Charles Follot, *Histoire du papier peint en France du XVIIe au XIXe siècle* (Paris: Éditions d'Art Charles Moreau, 1935), p. 70.
2. See Bernard Jacqué, "Wallpaper in the Royal Apartments at the Tuileries, 1789–1792," *Studies in the Decorative Arts* 13, no. 1 (Fall–Winter 2005–6).

Veüe de la Maison et Jardin de Mr. Titon Conseiller Secretaire du Roy seise au Faubourg St. Antoine rüe de Charone de montreuill. fait par Aveline avec Privilege du Roy

fleur-de-lis with the Revolutionary Phrygian cap, axes entwined with *faisceaux des Licteurs* (lictor's fasces), red, white, and blue ribbons and rosettes, wreaths of oak leaves, and even a sprinkling of Bastilles. Commoners, moving up the social ladder, could enjoy a feeling of luxury with a material adapted to all kinds of interiors.

Nevertheless the citizens of this new France did not disdain the decorative styles and fashions of the past: they continued to favor neoclassical motifs, flowers, chintzes, *Chinoiseries, arabesques*, flock paper and so forth.

Once the Terror came to an end, calm returned under the Directoire and Consulate, and the economy started up again. Exports were re-authorized in 1802. An intense desire

Grisaille scenes from *Les Métamorphoses d'Ovide* hung in continuity like a scenic *panoramique*. Private collection, France.

ABOVE Fragment of a border in the Etruscan style, made fashionable by the French royal family in the Tuileries Palace, wood-block printed by Réveillon. Private collection, United States (formerly Isabella Barclay Collection, New York).

FACING PAGE Fragment from the same decor as the preceding border, in *arabesque* style, with Antique-type sphinxes and medallions, French manufacturer, c. 1790. Private collection, United States (formerly Isabella Barclay Collection, New York).

ABOVE Salon at Schlossgut Schmidt in Hess, showing Etruscan-style wallpaper inspired by Arthur & Robert's décor for the Tuileries Palace, France, c. 1790. Musée du Papier Peint, Rixheim (photo: Geert Wisse).

FACING PAGE Plain blue wallpaper panel *unis pour unis* bordered with the floral garlands made fashionable by Marie-Antoinette in the dining room of the Tuileries Palace, attributed to Arthur & Grenard, late 18th century. Musée des Arts Décoratifs, Paris. Similar borders were used in the homes of Benjamin Franklin, Thomas Jefferson, and George Washington (the ballroom at Mount Vernon), as well as in Count Sheremetyev's Ostankino palace near Moscow.

66

LEFT *Arabesque* panels à *l'éventail* ("in a fan") featuring peacock feathers. This paper is similar to the ones hung in Moccas Court, Herefordshire, the manufacturer Réveillon, 1790. Musée du Papier Peint, Rixheim.

FACING PAGE *Réveillon arabesque* decor at Moccas Court, Herefordshire, 1790.

BELOW, LEFT *R*evolutionary wallpaper combining emblems of the French Republic (Gallic rooster, Phrygian cap, etc.) on a background of the tricolor flag, unknown French manufacturer. Musée Carnavalet, Paris.

BELOW, RIGHT *W*allpaper with emblems and mottoes of the French Revolution, unknown French manufacturer, c. 1790. Musée Carnavalet, Paris.

3. Madeleine Deschamps, *Empire* (New York: Abbeville Press, 1994), p. 83.

for pleasure reappeared, and high fashion made a comeback in certain circles. In Paris, the beautiful public parks—ruined during the Revolutionary riots—were restored, becoming sites for promenades, debates, celebrations, and attractions of various kinds. These gardens included the Tuileries, the Luxembourg, the Jardin des Plantes (Botanical Gardens), and the Palais-Royal, the latter referred to as the "first reopened salon." [3] Fashionable men (*incroyables*) and women (*merveilleuses*) strolled through the Palais-Royal or met for a drink at the Café du Grand Véfour, decorated with their lovely Pompeian-style painted mirror-panels.

Louis-Sébastien Mercier in his famous chronicle of late eighteenth-century Paris, *Tableau de Paris* (1781-90), describes the Palais-Royal courtyard as follows: "A unique spot on this globe. Visit London, Amsterdam, Madrid, or Vienna, you will see nothing like it. . . . It is called the capital of Paris. Everything can be found there. . . . This enchanted destination is a tiny, luxurious city enclosed in a larger one; it is a temple of sensuality where glittering vices banish any shadow of modesty: there is no open-air café in the world more lavishly depraved; when one laughs, innocence blushes. " Paris had become epitome of luxury—and the queen of the night.

Changes in taste and interior decoration under the Empire period provoked a real transformation of wallpaper.

Following Bonaparte's expedition to Egypt in 1798, a completely new style, "Egyptomania," became all the rage. Its new motifs included sphinxes, wigs, lotuses, and obelisks. The two surviving examples in Paris that best reflect this inventive style are the former private residence of Napoleon's empress, Joséphine de Beauharnais (now the German embassy), and the Hôtel de Brienne, home of his mother, Laetitia (now the French ministry of defense).

Inspired by periodicals of the day such as *La Mésangère*, women played a more active role in interior decoration, further encouraged by Joséphine, who personally influenced contemporary fashions: "Hardly had Her Imperial Majesty arrived in the capital that everything took on a new appearance."

RIGHT *Fragment of an* arabesque *pattern designed by Réveillon in 1789, reissued and block-printed on a brushed blue ground after 1792 by Jacquemart & Bénard, successors to Réveillon. Carolle Thibaut-Pomerantz Collection. The same Réveillon design on an ecru ground was used in the master bedroom of the Phelps-Hatheway House, Suffield, Connecticut.*

BOTTOM *Stamp of Jean-Baptiste Réveillon (RJB), Royal Manufactory, taken over by Jacquemart & Bénard, hand-dated 11 Messidor of the Revolutionary calendar, which establishes the impression after 1792. The number 692, also appearing on the bottom of the roll, indicates the year that Réveillon created the design (1789). Carolle Thibaut-Pomerantz Collection.*

ABOVE Wallpaper imitating a hanging sheer fabric called *Linon Batiste*, a specialty of Jacquemart & Bénard, patented in 1800, late 18th century. Musée du Papier Peint, Rixheim (formerly Follot Collection).

FACING PAGE, TOP *Linon Batiste* panel with Antique-style vases ringed by flowers on a hand-brushed pink ground, Jacquemart & Bénard, late 18th century. Carolle Thibaut-Pomerantz Collection. An example of this design is in the Bibliothèque Nationale de France, Paris.

FACING PAGE, BOTTOM Small frieze in the Etruscan style on a brushed black ground, attributed to Jacquemart & Bénard, late 18th century. Carolle Thibaut-Pomerantz Collection.

A new social class composed of bureaucrats and businessmen arose during the Empire, undertaking innovations and transformations of the country's major cities, public spaces, and private dwellings. The architects and decorators Charles Percier and Pierre Fontaine were commissioned to renovate Joséphine's Malmaison residence; in 1801 Percier and Fontaine became the government's official architects. Their *Recueil de Décorations Intérieures* (1812) long remained a source of inspiration for designers of furnishings throughout Europe. During a stay in England, Percier and Fontaine collaborated with their British counterpart, the well-known neoclassicist Robert Adam, working in the decorative arts, and, more particularly, on wall decoration. They demonstrated their talent by conveying all the pomp of the new Caesar, Napoleon I. Numerous examples of their work, typifying the Imperial style—the triumphal arch of the Carrousel in the Tuileries and the fountain of the Place du Châtelet, for example—are still to be found in Paris.

These prevailing trends, promoted in France by Percier and Fontaine and in England by Adam, further reinforced a preference for Antique-style decoration, inspired not only by the excavations at Pompeii but also by those in Rome and Etruria. Walls were decorated with large panels composed of *arabesques* and framed by pilasters, moldings, and friezes of diamond patterns and palmettes, as at Moccas Court in England and throughout France. This style was reflected in highly fashionable wallpapers manufactured by Jacquemart & Bénard and Arthur & Robert.

One novelty in wallpaper was the introduction of large friezes and borders. These were dense and richly colored, with varied motifs: heavy garlands of flowers and fruit, gilded acanthus leaves, stylized plants imitating bronze work, Greek palmettes, cameos, medallions, putti, bacchantes, and so forth. Of great size and presence, many were elegantly used as over-door panels. Trompe-l'oeil also came back into fashion, imitating materials such as wood, marble, and fabric.

Following Napoleon's accumulation of military victories and in light of his growing taste for display and grandeur, a more formal taste evoking the military, masculine style of ancient Rome became popular. The new decorative vocabulary included motifs such as winged Victories, wreathes, trophies, griffons, and lion-claw feet as well as luxurious draperies evocative of the wall hangings in Roman villas and military camps with their spears, gilded wreathes of laurel and oak, and heavy tassels, plus Napoleon's imperial emblems of the eagle and the bee. Colors are brilliant, emphasizing the red of Imperial cloaks. This taste for opulence was reflected in the design of wallpaper: Jacquemart & Bénard supplied the Imperial residences in Fontainebleau, Saint-Cloud, and Rambouillet, and in 1819 the firm decorated the private apartments of Empress Marie-Louise.

Thus interior decoration of the day was inspired by the pomp associated with this new victorious Caesar. These decorative attributes were, as the Duchess of Guermantes so rightly put it in Marcel Proust's *In Search of Lost Time*, "the chic of those who have so many victories that they spread their emblems throughout their interiors."

FACING PAGE *R*are wallpaper showing a medallion with a woman in Directoire dress (formerly ascribed to Louis-Léopold Boilly) surrounded by garlands of flowers, block-printed on a brushed ash-brown ground, French manufacturer, c. 1795. Musée des Arts Décoratifs, Paris (formerly Isabella Barclay Collection, New York).

PAGES 74-75 *Le Palais-Royal*, decor depicting imaginary gardens enlivened by strollers with "folies" or "fabriques", picturesque garden structures within arbors, pillars, and groves. This ensemble is considered a forerunner of scenic decors. Mounted on an eight-leaf screen, wood-block printed in grisaille on a hand-brushed blue ground. Designer and maker unknown, 1808–11 (according to fashion plates in *Le Journal des dames et des modes*, published by Pierre de La Mésangère). Musée du Papier Peint, Rixheim.

73

ABOVE *Original design by Percier and Fontaine for the decor Allégorie des Arts*. Musée des Arts Décoratifs, Paris.

FACING PAGE *The panel "Architecture" from the decor Allegorie des Arts*: wood-block printed and attributed
to Jacquemard & Bénard, c. 1797–1801, after a drawing by Percier & Fontaine. Provenance: Lasker Residence, Illinois,
designed by the architect David Adler and decorated by Frances Elkins, 1925. Private collection, New York.

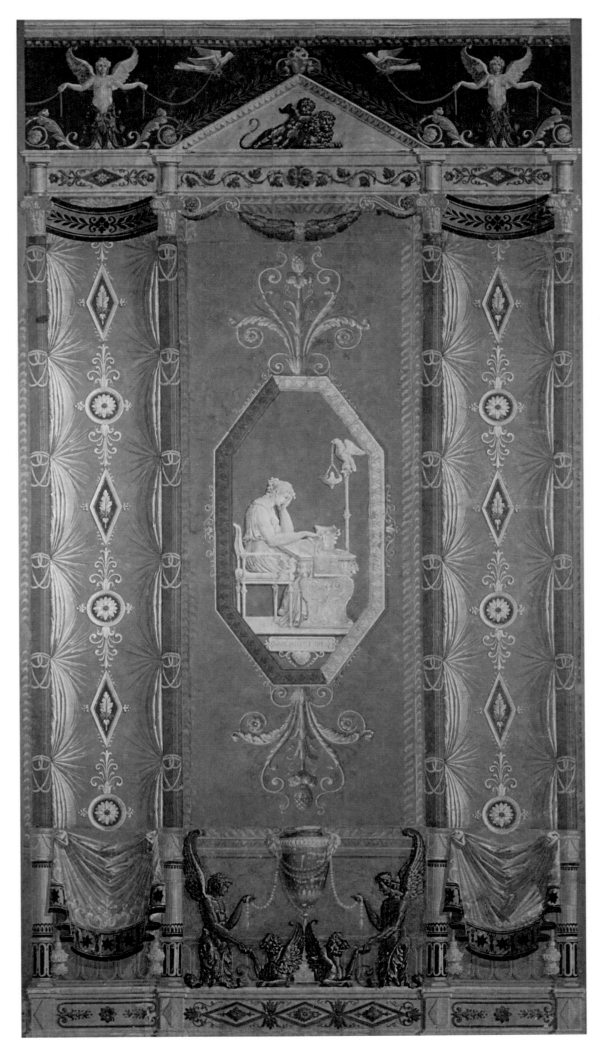

ABOVE *Flora* or *Springtime* allegory which inspired many French wallpaper designs in the late 18th and early 19th centuries; fresco from Ariane's Villa, 1st century B.C.E.-1st century C.E. . Museo Archeologico Nazionale, Naples.

FACING PAGE *A* canephore, or basket-bearing maiden, dressed in diaphanous drapery which suggests lightness and movement, finely hand-block printed in grisaille on a brushed blue ground, the manufacturer Jacquemart, 1815. Musée des Arts Décoratifs, Paris.

TOP *O*pulent frieze composed of bouquets in grisaille against green fans framed by gold acanthus leaves, attributed to Dufour, block-printed, 1810. Carolle Thibaut-Pomerantz Collection.

BOTTOM *L*arge frieze of cornucopia, scrollwork, and gold acanthus on imperial-red flocked ground, attributed to Dufour, c. 1810–20. Carolle Thibaut-Pomerantz Collection. The same paper is in the Deutsches Tapetenmuseum, Kassel (formerly Bernard Poteau Collection).

TOP *M*ilitary frieze with Greek helmet and sword, palmettes, and victory wreath, wood-block printed by Dufour, 1800–10. Bibliothèque Forney, Paris.

BOTTOM *O*pulent frieze with floral garlands, drapery, and imperial laurel wreath, wood-block printed by Dufour, c. 1810. Bibliothèque Forney, Paris.

ABOVE *Trompe-l'oeil* wallpaper of drapery gathered by gold trimmings, wood-block printed by Dufour, 1808. Blue Salon of Corvey Castle, Niedersachsen, Germany.

FACING PAGE *Sumptuous* drapery imitating white silk with rich gold trimmings on a red flocked ground, wood-block printed, attributed to Dufour, c. 1810. Musée des Arts Décoratifs, Paris (formerly Pierre-Yves Bonnet Collection).

83

THE GREAT ADVENTURE OF THE *PANORAMIQUE*

3

L'Histoire de Psyché et Cupidon,
by Joseph Dufour's chef d'oeuvre
dated 1816. Scenic wallpaper composed
of twelve tableaux, usually printed in
grisaille. This scene, "The Reconciliation
of Psyche and Venus," is one of the
rare examples printed in sepia-grisaille
tones for the first edition of 1816.
Carolle Thibaut-Pomerantz Collection.

During the Napoleonic Empire, wallpaper had won favor with the new aristocracy as well as the bourgeoisie. The wall—a surface that enveloped a real, limited space—vanished and was turned into a decor for illusion; the eye became accustomed to trompe-l'oeil effects. Actually, taste for trompe-l'oeil went back to a very old pictorial art, known as *quadratura* in Italy, found in Nero's Domus Aurea, and loggias painted by Raphael, Veronese, and Tiepolo. French artists revived this baroque mode of illusionism in the eighteenth century, as can been seen by the famous trompe-l'oeil colonnade painted on a blank wall at the royal residence in Marly; in Brunetti's decoration of the grand staircase of the Hôtel de Luynes; and in the Demarteau salon (the latter two reconstituted in the Musée Carnavalet in Paris). Also of note is the dining room of the hamlet at Chantilly, which, according to the memoirs of Baroness Oberkirch, was designed to entirely abolish any sense of walls.

That was when a new fashion—to be called *panoramique*—would become all the rage. This was due to the inventions of two artists, Carmontelle and Robert Barker.

Louis Carrogis (1717–1806), known as Carmontelle, was initially a topographical engineer, portrait painter, and garden designer famous for laying out the duc de Chartres' *folies* for his Monceau park in Paris in 1773. But he was above all the inventor, in 1785, of a process called "transparent": Enclosed in a small magical box lit from behind with candles, little transparent landscapes painted in gouache on Chinese or vellum paper, were unrolled as an animated continuous scene, giving an illusion of movement.

This ingenious system was, in fact, a continuation, in miniature, of what eighteenth-century architects had so adored: the panoramic views seen from a belvedere in a park or château, which contemporary engravings depicted from the point of view of a stroller on a promontory.

1. Monique Mosser, "The Taste for Bringing the Outside In," translated by Louise Guiney, in Odile Nouvel-Kammerer (ed.), *French Scenic Wallpaper, 1795–1865* (Paris: Flammarion/ Musée des Arts Décoratifs, 2000), p. 203.
2. François Robichon, "From Panoramas to Panoramic Wallpaper," translated by David Wharry, in Nouvel-Kammerer, *French Scenic Wallpaper*, p. 167.
3. Ibid, p. 168.
4. Ibid., p. 165.
5. Véronique de la Hougue attributes the design of *Les Métamorphoses d'Ovide* to Jean-Gabriel Charvet, and its manufacture to the La Charité workshop in Lyon, c. 1790, whereas Bernard Jacqué attributes it to the firm of Arthur & Robert in Paris.

Carmontelle explained his approach this way: "I attempted to [combine], in a single garden, all times and all places. This is no more than fantasy, the desire to have an extraordinary garden, purely for pleasure." [1]

Then, in 1787, the concept of the "panorama" was brought back into fashion by the Irish painter Robert Barker (1739–1806) with a process he designed to recreate the way the eye scans a natural landscape. "My invention, that I call 'nature in a glance' is intended, by means of certain drawings and paintings . . . to create a full and complete perspective of a place and its geographical setting as seen by an observer who looks all around it." [2]

Standing on a platform in a closed circular interior, whose walls were covered with painted canvases, viewers found themselves in the midst of a setting where the landscape and its horizon line extended in one continuous, total vision, completely abolishing the structure of the interior space to give the illusion of transposition beyond reality into a dream-like other-world. This spectacular invention of panorama sparked a veritable revolution and was enormously popular among the Parisian bourgeoisie: crowds flocked to the rotundas installed on Boulevard Montmartre in Paris in 1800, where the first panorama—"Paris seen from the central pavilion in the Tuileries" and "Toulon during the withdrawal of the English Fleet in 1793"—were exhibited.

The panorama was "a 'utopian' space in which the observer is both in a town and in the midst of nature, traveling and stationary, and finally both spectator and protagonist." [3]

The "panoramic view" was launched, and soon was embedded in the imaginative world of the time: it will inspire a new type of mural art for wallpapers, and pave the way for the so-called *panoramiques*. Henri Clouzot wrote in 1935, "Where did the idea for pictorial wall covering originate? One can, with complete certainty, trace it back to the success of the first panoramas. . . . As in these famous rotundas, the spectator—in this instance the apartment's occupant—finds himself in the midst of a picture whose horizon stretches all around him, as if he was on the top of a hill or a tall monument." [4]

The first large-scale decors, *Les Métamorphoses d'Ovide* (Ovid's Metamorphoses) and *Le Palais-Royal* (The Royal Palace) were precursors of a mural art form of an altogether different dimension. [5] Conceived as modular panels that could be adapted to any interior architectural context, these ensembles are treated as scenes linked by the joining of strips in a continuous but none-repetitive scheme, punctuated by columns, floral garlands, or arbors. This new art would soon reach its height with two geniuses: Joseph Dufour and Jean Zuber.

In 1797, Joseph Dufour (1754–1827), who had begun his career as a designer in Lyons, founded a wallpaper firm in Mâcon. There, shortly before 1804, he conceived the first decor in continuity—the true precursor of *panoramiques*—*Le Jardin Anglais* (The English Gardens, previously known as *Jardins de Bagatelle*), and designed by Pierre-Antoine Mongin. [6]

In 1804 Dufour created his first major *panoramique*, *Les Voyages du Capitaine Cook* (The Voyages of Captain Cook), also referred to as *Les Sauvages de la Mer Pacifique*, that he described as "paintings for wallpaper decoration." The design by Jean-Gabriel Charvet clearly called for a polychromatic treatment. Exhibited at the 1806 French Industrial Exposition at the Louvre, the work was widely noticed, and was greatly admired by the public, even though Dufour was not awarded a prize. As a contemporary critic commented:

> The new wall hangings, whose subjects taken from the voyages of Captain Cook, are perhaps the most curious example of this genre. Nothing, neither efforts, nor care, nor financial sacrifices, has discouraged Monsieur Dufour. He had innumerable difficulties to overcome, everything needed to be created; but he has finally achieved his aim and is about to benefit from the fruit of his long labors. [7]

This technical and financial challenge resulted in the largest printed decor ever executed. Stretching some 33 feet (10 meters) in length, printed on rag paper, it was composed of roughly a hundred colors applied by means of more than a thousand wood-blocks on a pale blue, hand-brushed ground.

Dufour and Charvet had gathered a good deal of documentation from Cook's accounts of voyages and the explorations of Bougainville, La Pérouse, and La Harpe. The sum of their knowledge was condensed into a single artistic composition that could be taken in at a glance. The *panoramique* was also inspired by Rousseau's idealized concept of the "noble savage." The interpretation was nevertheless highly European: the artist took liberties with the idyllic poses—recalling ballets in the operas of the day—and with dress, which is closer to that of the Directoire and Empire styles. Nonetheless, this vision lent the decor great charm and above all spurred curiosity about and interest in the customs of exotic lands. The myth of a distant paradise and the call to travel, themes which would be further developed, are already in evidence.

6. Catalog entry no. 78 in Nouvel-Kammerer, *French Scenic Wallpaper*, p. 308.
7. Georgette Pastiaux-Thiriat and Jean Pastiaux, *Un créateur de papiers peints, Joseph Dufour, 1754–1827*, exh. cat. (Tramayes: Syndicat d'Initiative de Tramayes, 2000).

As Dufour himself put it so well, "The goal of this undertaking was to please the eye and to stimulate the imagination without fatiguing it. . . . Everything that tends to embellish a home . . . has a goal, namely to encourage one to enjoy his interior." [8]

Dufour was a humanist, a generous man of modern views who believed in mutual exchange. "The more you give, the more you acquire," he said, running counter to his predecessors, who had jealously guarded their manufacturing secrets, never revealing the names of their artists. Driven by sincere educational and popularizing motives, he defended the idea that a *panoramique* should serve as a tool of instruction: "With little effort, almost unconsciously, a mother will be able to give history and geography lessons to an inquisitive, intelligent daughter." [9]

Encouraged by his success, Dufour opened a Paris factory in 1807, in a former abbey at 10, rue Beauvau in the Faubourg Saint-Antoine. In 1808 he hired a designer-engraver named Xavier Mader, who would later earn fame with his own firm. In that first year with Dufour, Mader designed *Les Portiques d'Athènes* (Athenian Porticoes), followed by *Les Galeries Mythologiques* (Mythological Galleries).

In 1816, at the end of the Empire period, Dufour produced his undisputed masterpiece, *L'Histoire de Psyché et Cupidon* (The Story of Psyche and Cupid), which won a silver medal at the French Industrial Exposition of 1819. Inspired by the painter François Gérard, the designs were done by Louis Laffitte and Merry-Joseph Blondel, and adapted life-size by Mader. This series, the only *panoramique* to show characters in an interior setting, comprises twelve distinct tableaux depicting the love of Psyche and Cupid, based on La Fontaine's story. Remarkable perspective hollows out the walls of the room, plunging the viewer into the poetic atmosphere of Palladian villas. The effects of shading and chiaroscuro grisaille are finely rendered, underscoring the range of tones in fabrics, draperies, and stone.

Dufour's other successful *panoramiques* included *Les Monuments de Paris* (Monuments of Paris, 1812); *Les Rives du Bosphore* (The Banks of the Bosphorus, 1812); *Les Fêtes Grecques ou Jeux Olympiques* (Greek Festivities [or Olympic Games], 1818); *Télémaque dans l'Île de Calypso*

8. Ibid.
9. Catalog entry no. 52 in Nouvel-Kammerer, *French Scenic Wallpaper*, p. 294.

RIGHT *D*etail from the panoramique *Paul et Virginie*, based on the novel by Bernardin de Saint-Pierre (1787), in grisaille or sepia tones, wood-block printed by Joseph Dufour, Paris, c. 1824. Deutsches Tapetenmuseum, Kassel.

FACING PAGE *A* panel from the decor *Le Jardin Anglais* hung as a painting. Cristina Carlini Collection, Paris.

PAGES 90-93 *Le Jardin Anglais*, also known as *Jardins de Bagatelle*, was one of the forerunners of scenic wallpapers was designed by Pierre Antoine Mongin and wood-block printed by Joseph Dufour in Mâcon before 1804. Carolle Thibaut-Pomerantz Collection.

PAGES 94-97 *Les Voyages du Capitaine Cook,* also known as *Les Sauvages de la Mer Pacifique,* was the first grand scale *panoramique* printed by Joseph Dufour in 1804 and designed by Jean-Gabriel Charvet. Private collection, Florida.

RIGHT *Le Brésil*, scenic wallpaper designed by Joseph Fuchs for Desfossé in 1862. Coming after Zuber's 1830 views of Brazil, it featured exotic birds and vegetation instead of human figures. Musée du Papier Peint, Rixheim.

FACING PAGE, TOP One panel from *Vues de Suisse*, the first scenic wallpaper produced by Jean Zuber, designed by Pierre-Antoine Mongin, 1804. This idealized "Suisse" was in fashion at the beginning of the 19th century. France, De Kergorlay Collection.

FACING PAGE, BOTTOM *Les Vues de Suisse*, in the salon of the Imperial Countess Hochberg, Schwetzingen Palace Collection, Bade-Wurtenberg, Germany.

(Telemachus on the Island of Calypso, 1818); *Les Incas ou la Destruction de l'Empire du Pérou* (The Incas, or the Destruction of the Peruvian Empire, 1818); *Le Voyage d'Anthénor* (Antenor's Travels, c. 1820); *Les Vues d'Italie* (Views of Italy, 1822); *Paul et Virginie* (Paul and Virginie, c. 1824); and *Renaud et Armide* (Rinaldo and Armida, illustrating the famous love affair in Tasso's *Jerusalem Delivered*, 1831). In 1821 Dufour took his son-in-law, Leroy, as a partner, thus becoming the firm of Dufour & Leroy, one of the largest wallpaper manufacturers of the day.

The other major pioneer of *panoramiques*, Jean Zuber (1773–1852), began his career in 1791 with Dollfus in Mulhouse; in 1802 he took over the Hartmann Risler firm in Rixheim, where he hired the talented Gobelins painter Joseph-Laurent Malaine, who had already worked for the leading eighteenth-century manufacturers.

In May 1804 Zuber produced his first *panoramique*, *Les Vues de Suisse* (Views of Switzerland), which he described as "a tableau in wallpaper" composed of sixteen strips printed in ninety-five colors using 1,084 wood-blocks. This paper was exhibited at the 1806 French Industrial Exhibition: "Zuber … has commissioned landscapes which present difficulties which have been overcome in such a way as to be useful to the progress of this art. The jury has awarded him a silver medal of the Second Class section." The "tableau" was a synthesis of various views of the Alps, a latter-day Arcadia evoking once again the pastoral serenity and power of the mountains so praised by Rousseau.

ABOVE *Les Muses*, a pair of panels designed by Xavier Mader and printed by Zuber, c. 1820. Carolle Thibaut-Pomerantz Collection. Other examples are in the Deutsches Tapetenmuseum, Kassel, and Musée des Arts Décoratifs, Paris.

FACING PAGE *Les Portiques d'Athènes* or *Didon et Énée*, the first scenic paper designed by Xavier Mader for Joseph Dufour, c. 1808. Musée des Arts Décoratifs, Paris.

ABOVE "*Psyche* Bringing the Fountain of Youth to Venus" interior decoration inspired by the neoclassical motifs of the panel. Carolle Thibaut-Pomerantz Collection.

FACING PAGE "*The* Fountain of Youth" revealing the finesse of the engraving and the rich shades of grisaille.

$\mathcal{L}$arge panel from the scenic wallpaper *Les Incas*, showing Pizarro's arrival in Peru, designed by Jean-François Marmontel, printed by Joseph Dufour, 1818.
Mr. and Mrs. Felipe Ortiz-Patino Collection, Geneva.

FACING PAGE *Scene* from the *panoramique* called *Les Rives du Bosphore* by Joseph Dufour, original edition before 1812. Private collection.

ABOVE *A* pair of panels from *Les Rives du Bosphore* by Joseph Dufour, original edition prior to 1812. In a setting with Mattia Bonetti's "Surf" sofa, 2006. Carolle Thibaut-Pomerantz Collection and Catberro Gallery, Paris.

PAGES 108-109 *The* "Glacial Seas" panel from *Les Zones Terrestres*, a *panoramique* designed by Eugène Ehrmann and printed by Zuber, 1855. This decor was produced until 1878; the "Glacial Seas" part is more rare. Private collection, Massachusetts.

ABOVE *Les Chasses de Compiègne*, designed by Carle Vernet for Jacquemart & Bénard, 1812–15. This scenic wallpaper is considered to be the finest created on the theme of hunting. This scene, the last, depicts a picnic gathering. Private collection, Paris.

FACING PAGE *Les Chasses de Compiègne*. Detail from the scene of the kill. Private collection, United States, (formerly from the private collection of Jean Zuber for the Commanderie in Rixheim, Alsace).

FACING PAGE *La Bataille d'Héliopolis*, also known as *Les Français en Égypte*, designed by Jean Julien Deltil, wood-block printed by the manufacturer Velay, Paris, 1818. This panel depicts the victory of General Kléber over the Ottomans at Heliopolis. Private collection, Paris.

ABOVE *La Bataille d'Austerlitz*, outstanding *panoramique* of "The Victory of Military Strategy." This panel shows Napoleon on Mount Pratzen flanked by his chiefs of staff. Attributed to the manufacturer Jourdan & Villar, 1827–29. Private collection.

ABOVE *Marcel* Proust's muse, Comtesse Greffulhe, who inspired the character of the Duchesse de Guermantes in *In Search of Lost Time*.

FACING PAGE *Scenic* wallpaper in sepia, titled *Campagne Romaine* (Roman Countryside), attributed to the Pignet company, Saint-Genis-Laval, c. 1820. Private collection, France (formerly in the home of the Comtesse Greffulhe, rue d'Astorg, Paris).

BELOW *Fragments* of the newspaper *Le Moniteur*, published in Kassel when Napoleon's brother Jérôme was king of Westphalia. These papers were used as backing for the scenic, *Procession Chinoise* now in the Deutsches Tapetenmuseum, Kassel.

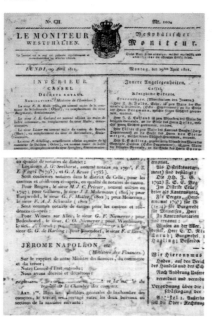

Later Zuber was inspired by ancient Greece and Rome, and exotic lands, as seen in *Les Zones Terrestres* (Terrestrial Zones, 1854) and *Le Brésil* (Brazil, 1860), reproducing the local flora and fauna with an abundance of colors. The interest in landscapes and bright colors led to the steady elimination of human figures in favor of Edenic jungle foliage and various evocations of paradise.

At the same time, Zuber turned to more "modern" subjects. Fascinated by the misty landscapes described by Sir Walter Scott, he produced *Les Vues d'Écosse* (Views of Scotland, or Lady of the Lake, 1827), an exemplary subject for budding Romantics; indeed, Zuber's *panoramiques* reflected the *Sturm und Drang* sensibility of pre-romantic German literature. The struggle for Greek independence inspired *Vues de la Grèce Moderne* (Views of Modern Greece, or The Greek Battles) designed by Jean-Julien Deltil (successor to Mongin, who died in 1807). A series showing the other side of the Atlantic, *Les Vues de l'Amérique du Nord* (Views of North America, 1834) would be revised and updated in 1852, and entitled *La Guerre de l'Indépendance Américaine* (The American War of Independence).

In the first half of the nineteenth century, the Dufour and Zuber firms were among the most prestigious wallpaper manufacturers of *panoramiques*—and the most prolific.

In the mood of this romantic nineteenth century, the vogue of *panoramiques* was enhanced by the urge to travel and the taste of adventure brought to fashion by the large paintings of this period. The art of wallpaper was no longer limited to patterns of *arabesques*, figurines, curves and interlacing flowers : landscapes, distant lands, history, mythology, and literature to cover the interiors. Decors were not merely decorative, but meaningful.

Several other noteworthy manufacturers contributed to the field, such as Jacquemart & Bénard, known for the famous *Chasses de Compiègne* (Hunting scenes in the forest of Compiègne), designed by Carle Vernet. Sauvinet created *Les Vues de Lyon* (Views of Lyons) a work that was presented at the 1825 French Industrial Exhibition. The Velay firm issued *La Bataille d'Héliopolis* (The Battle of Heliopolis, also known as The French in Egypt), *La Grande Chasse au Tigre dans l'Inde* (Tiger Hunting in India), and *Réjouissances Populaires aux Champs Élysées à l'Occasion de la Fête du Roi* (Public Festivities on the Champs-Élysées for the King's Feast Day). The Pignet factory in Saint-Genis-Laval produced an ambitious *Rome-Paris-London* scenic printed in shades of sepia, while the famous *Bataille d'Austerlitz* (Battle of Austerlitz, c. 1827) is attributed to the Jourdan & Villar manufacture.

Other beautiful *panoramique* ensembles survive from this period, but attribution and dating are often uncertain, given the loss of many archives, as is the case, for example, of *Procession Chinoise* (Chinese Procession, c. 1811–20) and *Le Passage des Détroits* (Passage through the Straits, c. 1820).

Thus these most original creations introduced a totally new mural art, one that remained unique to French manufacturers and established itself as the art of "fine engraving at a grand scale." The *panoramique* opened a window onto limitless worlds, totally obliterating walls. Clearly it acted as a "trompe-l'oeil"—it fooled the eye—but it also recounted, delighted, and brought an exotic touch to the most fashionable *salons*.

Meanwhile, steady technical advances favored the production of wallpaper: the copper printing cylinder was developed in 1827, continuous paper rolls in 1830, and rotary presses in the 1840s.

The rise of industrial exhibitions also had a significant impact. These shows, supported by Napoleon in their aim to promote French arts and industry, awarded prizes in an effort to inspire exhibitors to greater excellence. The 1806 French Industrial Exhibition was crucial to the success of Dufour and Zuber, while the one in 1819 marked the triumph of *panoramiques*. The first Great Exhibition was held at the Crystal Palace in London, in 1851. English manufacturers of wallpaper received favorable notice there once again, but the French outdid them and received all the awards, the top prize notably going to the firm of Étienne Delicourt.

PAGE 116 *Paris-Rome-London*, scenic depicting a view of London with the north bank of the Thames, the City, the Church of Saint Mary on the Strand, Somerset House, and Waterloo Bridge. The manufacturer Pignet, Saint-Genis-Laval, France, 1853. Private collection, New York.

PAGE 117 *Scene* from the *panoramique* called *Procession Chinoise*, wood-block printed in sepia. French, unknown manufacturer. c. 1810-1820. Private collection, New York.

ABOVE *Scènes Turques*, sepia-grisaille scenic, unknown designer, but based on drawings by Jean-Baptiste Hilaire for Comte Choiseul-Gouffier and attributed to the manufacturer Dufour, c. 1815. Private collection.

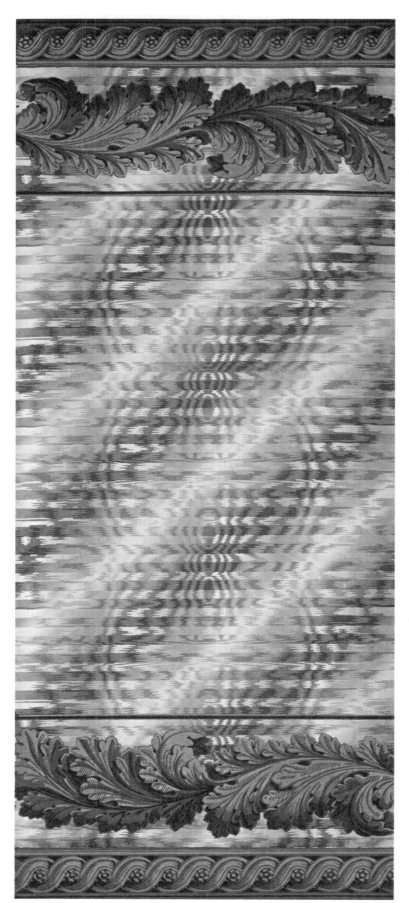

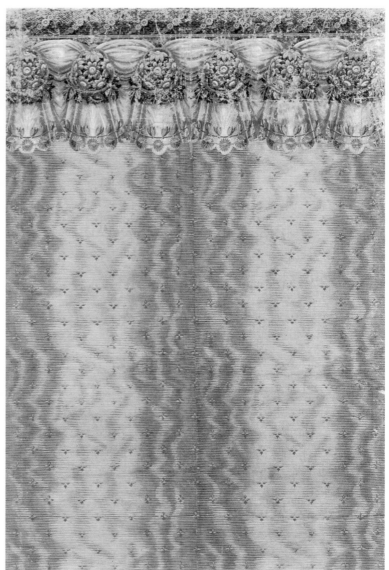

LEFT *Irisé* (iridescent-like) panel by Jean Spoerlin, who invented the technique in 1819 for Zuber, c. 1820. Musée du Papier Peint, Rixheim.

ABOVE *Panel* by Johann-Christian Arnold, German manufacturer based in Kassel, who was inspired by French wallpapers, imitating drapery and "moiré" silks, dated 1821. Deutsches Tapetenmuseum, Kassel.

FACING PAGE *Iris* wallpaper panel, printed by Zuber, c. 1820. Deutsches Tapetenmuseum, Kassel.

ABOVE *Decor Grandes Chasses* (Great Hunts) designed by Antoine Dury,
printed by Étienne Délicourt, Paris, awarded a gold medal at the Great
Exhibition of London, 1851. Musée des Arts Décoratifs, Paris.

The Exposition Universelle held in Paris in 1855 was a major event given the presence of Jules Desfossé, then considered the finest manufacturer of the Second Empire. Desfossé hired well-known artists, including Wagner, Poterlet, and Fuchs. Having inherited the collection of designs and blocks made by Mader, Desfossé went into partnership in 1863 with his brother-in-law and founded Desfossé & Karth, which bought Dufour's valuable stock in 1865, thereby placing the firm at the summit of a veritable empire. During the 1855 Exposition Universelle, Desfossé set up a remarkable stand that featured three major works by contemporary artists. He turned first to Thomas Couture, with whom he devised an iconographic theme: "Vices and Virtues." Couture executed his tableau *Les Prodigues* (also known as *Souper de Pierrot*). Then Desfossé turned to Édouard Müller, known as "Rosenmüller", the painter of roses, who designed *Le Jardin d'Armide* (Armida's Garden), and, finally, to Auguste Clésigner, who created *L'Automne ou la Bacchante Endormie* (Autumn, or the Sleeping Bacchante). These "tableau" panels, in amazing colors, were the result of highly technical advances: *Les Prodigues* was printed on two very large assembled papers, while *Le Jardin d'Armide* required more than three thousand blocks to produce. These formidable creations earned Desfossé a first-class medal.

Le Jardin d'Armide could be considered the absolute masterpiece of the floral genre. Müller incorporated a multitude of different kinds of flowers into a magnificent, enchanting garden, in which a single marble statue—a reproduction of James Pradier's *Pandora*—fades behind a profusion of colors. This garden (the inspiration for Klingsor's magic garden in Richard Wagner's opera *Parsifal*) represents the ultimate refinement of the highly original art of illusionist decors, an invitation to dream as well as a compendium of knowledge, in that botanists reproduced the flora with an exactness worthy of encyclopedic plates.

A new fashion was gaining ground, namely for *jardins d'hiver* (indoor gardens), hothouses, and verandas, which would strongly influence wallpaper design. It would leave its mark on decoration in the Second Empire, as seen in the famous residence of Princess Mathilde, cousin to Napoleon III. The princess would show off her lavish *jardin d'hiver* in her *hôtel particulier* on rue de Courcelles in Paris, much the same way that Louis XIV had invited his guests to discover the parks of Versailles.

Couture's *Les Prodigues* also made a strong impression. Set in the early hours after an evening of debauchery, the picture is as striking as a scene from *La Traviata*. Looking like the commedia dell'arte character, with his billowing white sleeves, the lovesick Pierrot sits wearily on a table. This work displays both boldness and power, being at once a distant echo of William Hogarth's painting *Marriage A-la-mode* and a harbinger of the tearful Pierrot in Marcel Carné's film *Les Enfants du Paradis* (*Children of Paradise*). It is also the only known wallpaper to be signed by both artist and manufacturer. Desfossé imparted a new dimension to wallpaper at this 1855 exhibition, enabling the medium to rival painting and win acceptance as an art in its own right.

These works reveal the extent to which wallpaper design, right up to the end of the Second Empire, sought inspiration in the past, or in painting of the day. Yet it gradually became obvious that the panoramic enlargement of a painting was not the right path to take during a golden age in which the renewal of painting itself was forcing people to think about the originality of the creative act. The great art of the *panoramique*, a synthesis of painterly art and industrial skill, would inevitably be the object of criticism if it extended beyond that framework. What transformed the atmosphere of a room was not an oversized painting, but an artistic ensemble, prefiguring decorative art of the great interior designers, to be known as *ensembliers*.

Wallpaper nevertheless remained one of the most favored forms of mural art. With an increasingly wealthy society and the explosion of construction, it offered infinite possibilities to reflect the eclectic tastes of this fin-de-siècle period.

TOP *Lucullus*, wood-block printed in sepia or grisaille. This large frieze ran above the panel of *L'Automne* (above right) on Jules Desfossé's stand at the Exposition Universelle held in Paris in 1855. Carolle Thibaut-Pomerantz Collection.

ABOVE *L'Automne*, or *La Bacchante Endormie*, designed by Auguste Clésinger for Desfossé for the Exposition Universelle of 1855. Musée des Arts Décoratifs, Paris.

FACING PAGE *Les Prodigues*, or *Le Souper de Pierrot à la Maison d'Or*, specially designed for Desfossé by Thomas Couture; most unusually, Couture signed this work, as well as depicting himself as the Pierrot character. He executed other, smaller oil versions of this subject. Private collection, United States. Other examples of this panel are in the Musée des Arts Décoratifs, Paris; Musée du Papier Peint, Rixheim; and Art Institute of Chicago.

Le Jardin d'Armide, the central panel of Desfossé's stand
at the Exposition Universelle of 1855. Designed by Édouard Müller,
"the painter of roses," it is a masterpiece of floral depiction in a magical
garden. Private collection, United States. Other examples are in the
Musée des Arts Décoratifs, Paris; Deutsches Tapetenmuseum, Kassel;
and The Art Institute of Philadelphia.

PAGE 131, TOP LEFT "Japonisme" style panel, intermingling American scenery of the Brooklyn Bridge and Niagara Falls. Cooper-Hewitt National Design Museum, New York.

PAGE 131, TOP RIGHT Fragment of an embossed paper, called "Lincrusta-Walton," linoleum imitating faux stucco, material invented by the English manufacturer Lincrusta-Walton in 1877, pattern designed by Christopher Dresser, 1884. Cooper-Hewitt National Design Museum, New York (formerly in John D. Rockefeller Jr. residence on Fifth Avenue, New York).

PAGE 131, BOTTOM LEFT Trompe l'oeil wallpaper of a hanging kilim carpet, French manufacture, c. 1880. Sara Pura Weinheimer Collection, New York. Another such panel is conserved at the Deutsches Tapetenmuseum, Kassel, Germany.

PAGE 131, BOTTOM RIGHT Japonais, rich polychrome panel, wood-block printed by Desfossé & Karth, on a hand-brushed grey-and-white ground, 1880. The fashion for Japonisme style was launched at the Exposition Universelle of Paris in 1878. Musée des Arts Décoratifs, Paris.

PAGE 130, TOP LEFT Trompe l'œil of a Byzantine style mosaic wall, wood-block printed, French manufacturer, c. 1880–90. Deutsches Tapetenmuseum, Kassel, Germany (former Bernard Poteau collection).

PAGE 130, TOP RIGHT Babylone, wood-block printed decor by Defossé & Karth, c. 1880, Musée du Papier Peint, Rixheim.

PAGE 130, BOTTOM LEFT Wallpaper imitating a Louis XV-style gilt embroidery on a "moiré" silk ground, designed by Paul Balin, c. 1870–80, printed by A. Hans & Fils, France. Musée du Papier Peint, Rixheim (the museum possesses over 200 wallpapers by Balin).

PAGE 130, BOTTOM RIGHT Embossed and gilt wallpaper by Paul Balin, fine specialist of faux leathers and fabrics, c. 1870–80, printed by Alfred Hans & Fils. Bibliothèque Forney, Paris.

ABOVE, TOP Princess Mathilde's Dining Room on rue de Courcelles, by Charles Giraud, 1854. This oil painting illustrates the mid-19th-century vogue for indoor gardens. Château de Compiègne Collection.

ABOVE, BOTTOM Le Jardin d'Hiver (Winter Garden, dado section of this decor), designed by Édouard Müller for Desfossé. This wallpaper, produced in 1851, was a precursor of Defossé's Le Jardin d'Armide. United States. Decor by Ronald Bricke, New York.

WALLPAPER IN AMERICA

4

Ipswich wallpaper designed and printed by Thomas Strahan of Boston, commemorating the American Independence: Britannia mourns over a tomb flanked by figures representing America and the Declaration of Independence, all organized around the typical English "pillar and arch" motif, c. 1785–90. Cooper-Hewitt National Design Museum, New York.

In the early eighteenth century, pre-Revolutionary America was still an English colony. Undergoing rapid transformations, this young "New Frontier" was seeking to define itself, and irrespective of its political preoccupations, aspired to establish a certain quality of life. Although the immigrants considered the New World a promised land, memories of Europe were still very present in their minds.

America's most important exchanges at this time occurred with England and France who played very different roles: the former was a colonizing power, the latter a liberating one. France had been friendly to the "new continent" since the reign of Louis XVI, and had backed American efforts to free itself from English control. Trade was dominated by England, which protected its markets by passing various Trade and Navigation acts, providing many of America's essential resources, and thus influencing the local lifestyle. A taste for everything English would continue, out of habit, but did not prevent the development of new influences.

America displayed an interest in wallpaper from the early 1700s: easy to ship and not too expensive, it conveyed a sense of good taste and a note of European fashion. Imports from England and France spurred steady growth in business for wallpaper suppliers. Paper merchants and hangers advertised a varied range of "painted papers," (a translation of the French term) including papier-mâché, marbled or gilded papers, and imitation fabrics. Over the course of the eighteenth century a new profession slowly developed, although American production—through lack of know-how and raw materials—continued to be less accomplished in terms of both quality and style. European papers thus remained in favor. As in Europe, these sheets were first used to line small items of furniture or books

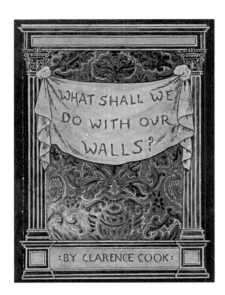

1. Catherine Lynn, *Wallpaper in America, from the Seventeenth Century to World War One* (New York: Cooper-Hewitt National Design Museum/W. W. Norton & Company, Inc., 1980), p. 93.

(which is why they were also called lining papers or endpapers), and were also designed as a substitute for more costly fabric wall hangings for a more modest clientele.

The first American wallpaper factory was owned by Plunkett Fleeson of Philadelphia (originally from either London or Dublin), active from 1739 to 1783, to judge by advertisements in the *Pennsylvania Gazette*. However, between 1740 and 1776, the evolving taste of more affluent Americans, prosperous merchants or gentry, tended to follow European fashions. Consequently, the demand for imported papers from Paris and London continued to grow.

The number of American producers (known as paper stainers or paper hangers) increased steadily in the last quarter of the century. Local competition began to have an impact with their more aggressive and "patriotic" advertisements. To protect and encourage the development and commercial success of these new American wallpaper manufacturers, after the War for Independence, a tax was imposed on imported papers in 1789. Americans exploited this situation by stressing the inexpensiveness—rather than the quality—of their products. The major merchants nevertheless continued to sell products imported from France and England, which were still much more refined and still in demand. The most fashionable wallpapers were flocked with baroque damask or velvet-like patterns, the English Gothic style (notably the "pillar and arch" design), as well as Chinese papers (called "India" papers) which the British introduced to the American market.

After the American Revolution, in 1776, the importation of English papers diminished and it was henceforth the French, recognized as superior in terms of paper quality, design, and color, who dominated the market and attracted the most sophisticated customers. Benjamin Franklin is known to have written to his wife in 1765, after having spent time in London and Paris, of his desire to use "plain papers" of solid blue with a border of flowers, *à la française* (in French style). George Washington also used these to decorate the ballroom at Mount Vernon. Thomas Jefferson, who succeeded Franklin as the American ambassador to France (1785–89), visited the finest workshops there and asked his agent, William Short, to send him samples of *arabesque* papers by Arthur & Robert. In 1790 Jefferson ordered plain-colored wallpaper, borders, and trompe-l'oeil papers of draperies and walls ("faux" walls). A true connoisseur and man of taste who could be considered one of the first trendsetters, Jefferson's purchases influenced the use of wallpaper in refined circles.

From Boston to Charleston, the fashion for wallpaper thus swept through grand New England families and Southern patricians. Thanks to a dynamic maritime trade, East Coast cities were able to stay abreast of foreign trends. Cities further inland would have to wait until the construction of railroads. People selected the finest examples of a unique type of mural decoration to lend a note of elegance and originality to their homes. As a contemporary English visitor observed, "The principal rooms which are of good dimensions are covered with French papers, which are chiefly used in this country, the patterns being much more beautiful, elegant and lively, than those manufactured in and exported from England, and surely much cheaper in proportion to their value."[1] Advertisements for papers produced, for example, by Francis Delorme in 1790, and Burrill and Edward Carnes (both based in Philadelphia) indicate Americans also showed an interest in revolutionary subjects.

From 1815 on, prosperous Americans developed a passion for the French specialty, *panoramiques*. The early best sellers were Dufour's *Les Monument de Paris*, *Les Rives du Bosphore*, *Les Voyages du Capitaine Cook*, and *Paysage de Télémaque dans l'Île de Calypso*, as well as Zuber's *Les Vues de Suisse*, *L'Hindoustan*, and *Les Vues d'Italie*. Americans were completely taken by these totally unique, vast compositions of such diverse themes. They often had several sets in their homes, and sometimes panels from different *panoramiques*

Wallpaper from the series *Grands Hommes* (America's Heroes) showing George Washington, one of four life-size portraits of heroes of the American Revolution (Benjamin Franklin, Thomas Jefferson, Marquis de Lafayette), produced by Jules Desfossé for the American market, 1856–57. Cooper-Hewitt National Design Museum, New York.

SACRED
TO
WASHINGTON

would be combined into one decor. *Panoramiques* were so successful in this vast, swiftly changing market that the two most important manufacturers, Dufour and Zuber, established their own representatives in America. A few *panoramiques* were even specifically created for this new clientele, such as Zuber's *Vues d'Amérique du Nord*, which was reworked for political reasons in 1852 and renamed *Scenes of the American Independence*, an ever-popular theme.

Extremely handsome *panoramiques*, vestiges of a style of interior decoration made fashionable by the country's elite, can still be found in many American homes, some of which have been listed as historic monuments. In New England, for instance, several homes in Portsmouth, New Hampshire—a major sea-trading town—were adorned with these sumptuous decors:

The Moffat-Ladd House (an Historic New England House, or HNE) features not only Zuber's *Vues d'Italie* but also English wallpapers with Gothic motifs and hunt scene engravings, *In Full Chase,* in the style of an English print room.

The Sarah Orne Jewett House (HNE) in South Berwick, Maine, is even more luxurious.

Hamilton House (HNE), also in South Berwick, has English "pillar and arch" papers similar to those in the house where Paul Revere lived during the American Revolution.

The Dorothy Quincy House (HNE) in Quincy, Massachusetts, features an elegant decor of neoclassical *arabesques* which Dorothy's father imported specially from France for his daughter's 1775 wedding to John Hancock, the first signer of the Declaration of Independence and first governor of the Commonwealth of Massachusetts.

A house in Montpelier, Vermont, has a set of Dufour's *Les Rives du Bosphore,* mounted on the walls in honor of a visit from Lafayette in 1825.

In Lindens Home in Danvers, Massachusetts, General Gage installed panels intermingling scenes from the decor *Les Incas, Paysage de Télémaque dans l'Île de Calypso,* and *Les Voyages d'Anthénor,* all by Dufour.

Marblehead, Massachusetts, a large East Coast trading town, is notable for the Jeremiah Lee Mansion, built circa 1767–69 by a wealthy merchant who became one of the richest men in the colonies. Lee ordered English hand-painted papers imitating large Panini-style paintings of ruins framed by Pillement-style *arabesques* and edged with block-printed borders that imitated stucco. These decors of ruins are identical to those once installed in the home of Stephen van Renssalaer in Albany, New York, and now in the collection of the Metropolitan Museum of Art, in New York. These wallpapers were erroneously attributed to the English papermaker John Baptist Jackson of Battersea.[2]

Oliver Phelps-Hatheway, a prosperous speculator from Suffield, Connecticut, imported in 1797 some of Réveillon's finest wallpapers, namely five varieties of neoclassical Pompeian decors printed by Jacquemart & Bénard, Réveillon's successors. Today one of these decors has been reinstalled in the "Federal Parlor" of the former residence of Henry Francis Du Pont, now the Winterthur Museum in Wilmington, Delaware.

In Providence, Rhode Island, Bruce Merriman hung a wonderful set of Chinese wallpapers showing scenes of everyday life such as people growing tea and rice or making porcelain. These papers, henceforth known as the "Beauport-Merriman Papers," were purchased in Canton in 1784 by an American trader, Eshing Green, on behalf of the paper merchant Robert Morris, and brought back on the first American vessel, the *Empress of China*. They remained in crates, totally intact, until roughly 1925, when the architect-decorator Henry Sleeper hung some of them in the ballroom of Merriman's mansion; the rest were hung at Beauport, a house built by Sleeper in Gloucester, Massachusetts. A few years ago, the papers in the Bruce Merriman home were transferred to the Peabody Museum in Salem, Massachusetts.

FACING PAGE *Sacred to Washington,* wallpaper with the allegories of Liberty and Justice, framed by the "pillar and arch" motif, wood-block printed in grisaille on a blue ground by Ebenezer Clough, Boston, c. 1800. The same wallpaper was used in the residence of governor Isaac Tichenor in Bennington, Vermont. Cooper-Hewitt National Design Museum, New York.

2. *Ibid.,* p. 55.

BELOW *Les Monuments de Paris*, a *panoramique* aligning the most beautiful buildings of the city , in this panel, the Pantheon, column of the Place Vendôme, and the Hôtel de Ville (City Hall) in a bucolic setting. Wood-block printed by Dufour, original edition of 1812–14. Private collection, United States.

FACING PAGE *Les Monuments de Paris* decor from the residence of William Clayton Williams, Richmond, Virginia. Reconstructed period room in the Metropolitan Museum, New York.

John Quincy Adams, president of the United States from 1825 to 1829, was a great *amateur* of wallpapers and in 1818 imported Zuber's *Vues d'Italie* and *Les Saisons* (The Seasons).

In the state of New York, Martin Van Buren, who was president from 1837 to 1841, chose Zuber's *Paysage de Chasse* (Hunting Scenes, 1832) for Lindenwald, his estate in Kinderhook, New York.

The Wright-Pomar House in Rose, New York, is an elegant little Italian-style residence built in 1856; the walls were lined with a series of portraits specially designed for the American market by the Jules Desfossé firm in 1856–57. Entitled *Les Grands Hommes* (Great Heroes), it included portraits of George Washington, Benjamin Franklin, Thomas Jefferson, and the Marquis de Lafayette.

In Pennsylvania, the Governor's Mansion in Harrisburg, where the state governor resides, is a modern reconstruction of an eighteenth-century Georgian-style English house. Its *salon* features the *panoramique, Les Incas* (Dufour, 1818). Gracie Mansion, the official residence of the mayor of New York City, was decorated with *Les Jardins Français* (French Gardens).

In the South, the reception hall of the Viscaya, Florida, former residence of James Deering, an important American industrialist, was hung with Dufour's *Galeries Mythologiques*, designed by Mader.

Longue Vue, just outside New Orleans, Louisiana, was the home of Edgar Bloom Stern and Edith Rosenwald Stern, department-store heirs and famous art patrons from the 1930s until the late 1970s; the upper hall was furnished around Félix Sauvinet's scenic *Vues de Lyon* (Views of Lyons, 1823), purchased from Nancy McClelland by Ellen Biddle Shipman, the early twentieth-century landscape gardener who designed the magnificent grounds of Longue Vue.

The Hermitage, near Nashville, Tennessee, was the estate of Andrew Jackson, a self-made man from the Far West, who became a great war hero, founder of the Democratic Party, and president from 1829 to 1837. The grand entrance hall of this typical fine Southern home displays *Paysage de Télémaque dans l'Île de Calypso* (Dufour, 1818), a *panoramique* that was ordered in 1836 from Robert Golder, a Philadelphia-based maker of wallpaper.

LES MUSES.

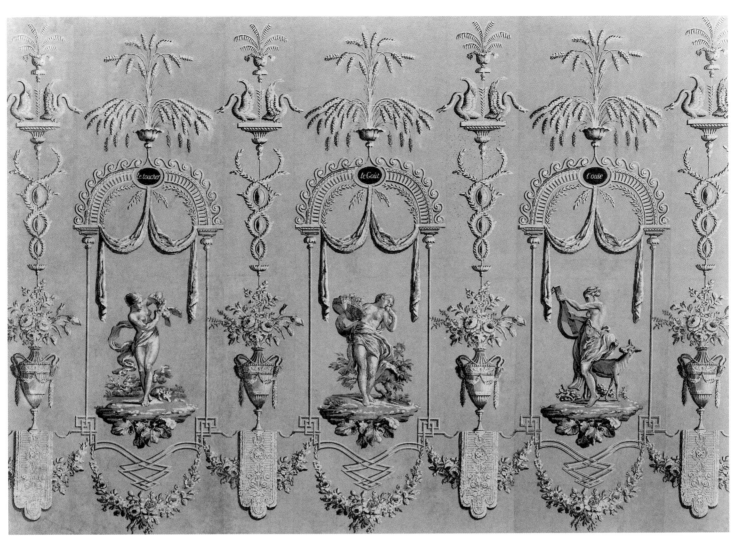

FACING PAGE, LEFT *E*xample of an *India Paper* inspired by Pillement and very fashionable in America. French manufacturer, c. 1760-65. Cooper-Hewitt National Design Museum, New York. (Gift of Eleanor and Sarah Hewitt).

FACING PAGE, RIGHT *C*hinese wallpaper with tree of life and birds. Typically, the design and colors are densest at the bottom, becoming lighter at the top. Canton school, early 19th century. Panel displayed at the Bruce Museum of Arts and Science, Greenwich, Connecticut, for the *China Trade in New England exhibition* (October 2004–March 2005). Carolle Thibaut-Pomerantz Collection.

Woodlawn, in Richmond, Kentucky, is a splendid antebellum plantation where Colonel William Rodes lived. The *panoramique* called *Chasses de Compiègne* (Hunting near Compiègne) was given to him around 1818 by General Cassius Clay on the occasion of his marriage to Clay's daughter. Ordered from the dealer Downing & Grant in Kentucky, the wallpaper was delivered directly from France by craftsmen from Jacquemart & Bénard who handled the hanging in the couple's new residence. It was finished in time for the reception held by the Clay and Rodes families in honor of General Lafayette during his farewell tour of America. Later taken down, the *panoramique* survived several moves until the families' descendants donated it to the Governor William Owsley House Museum in Kentucky, just a few miles from its original home.

Thus the extensively exported French *panoramiques*, by offering an invitation to travel, traveled widely themselves, and provided Americans with a magical opportunity to dream as well.

American interest in wallpaper continued into the twentieth century, notably during the 1920s, when a new elite brought it back into fashion. Wealthy families competed among themselves to create sumptuous interiors, and wallpaper decors were considered the epitome of good taste.

Major figures in the decorative arts influenced the fashions of the day, notably including the decorators Henry Sleeper, Frances Elkins (sister of the architect David Adler), and Nancy McClelland. The latter, having lived in Paris from 1907 to 1913, opened the first decorating and antiques department in a major department store, Wanamaker's, in New York in 1913, naming it *Au Quatrième* (On the Fourth Floor). In 1922 she opened her own store on East 57th Street in New York, offering French furnishings, *boiseries* (wood-paneling), wallpaper decors, and *panoramiques*. She not only sold historic wallpapers, but also reprinted some by wood-blocks and launched her own lines based on old samples, both French and American. Some of her reprints were used to renovate historic sites such as Colonial Williamsburg and Mount Vernon.

This great lady of decoration was thus responsible for hanging splendid French wallpaper decors in some of the most prestigious American homes. A true pioneer in the field, McClelland published the first reference work on the subject, *Historic Wallpapers* in 1924. In her preface, she particularly thanked her French friends Charles and Frances Huard, who introduced her to this marvelous world, Charles Follot, who allowed her to view his father's considerable collection, and finally Henri Clouzot, great connoisseur and director of the Musée Galliera in Paris. In the introduction to his own book, Clouzot ended with this tribute to McClelland: "In France—the cradle of wallpaper—no overview of wallpaper's history exists. Miss McClelland, by paying a veritable tribute, in America, to this art which is so charming yet so little known, provides what we hope is a salutary lesson to the French, and once again open their eyes to the treasures of their own country."[3] France honored McClelland in 1930 by investing her with the rank of Chevalier de la Légion d'Honneur.

In 1931 McClelland was one of the original members of the American Institute of Decorators (AID) and the founder of its New York branch. When she was named the winner of the first Justin Alleman Award for innovative wallpaper by members of the Wallpaper Wholesalers Association in 1946, it was stated that she, "alone among the decorating fraternity, fought against the use of plain walls. She started to use fine old documentary papers and turned the tide back to good taste. She made the wallpaper industry lift itself by its boot straps."[4]

Later McClelland herself would write, "I often think, when I see papered rooms, which many people put on very much as they put butter on bread. . . . What a pity, when there are dozens of interesting ways in which paper can be used—all of which enhance the value of the paper and the decorative feeling that it creates. No other minor art has done so much to beautify our homes."[5] After a brilliant career, the "first lady of wallpapers" died in 1959.

3. Henri Clouzot and Charles Follot, *Histoire du papier peint en France du XVIIᵉ au XIXᵉ siècle* (Paris: Éditions d'Art Charles Moreau, 1935), Introduction.
4. *New York Herald Tribune*, October 11, 1946.
5. *Wallpaper and Wallcoverings* 44 (November 1959).

FACING PAGE *Les Vues de Lyon*, scenic wood-block printed by Sauvinet, Paris, 1823, and hung in the Stern family's Longue Vue residence in New Orleans, Louisiana.

The Franco-American couple of Baron Charles and Frances Wilson Huard also largely contributed to promoting interest in French wallpapers in the United States. Charles Huard was a talented draftsman and dealer who briefly represented Nancy McClelland. He joined forces with Louis Chasset and his son Jean-Louis—antique dealers, restorers, and wallpaper printers—to recreate historic decors, such as the Palais-Royal in 1924. The Huards sold their important collection of wallpaper to the Museum of the Rhode Island School of Design in 1934.

The great art lover and patron Henry Francis Du Pont assembled a vast collection of American decorative arts, as well as Chinese, French, and English wallpapers, which became the foundation for his remarkable Winterthur Museum in Delaware. Du Pont was also a key promoter and member of the board of the Cooper Union Museum in New York, the first American museum devoted to wallpaper (now the Cooper-Hewitt National Design Museum). "My father's love of color led to his fondness for wallpaper," wrote his daughter, Ruth Lord, in her biography of Du Pont.[6]

In 1961, Du Pont accepted Jacqueline Kennedy's invitation to join a committee to advise her on redecorating the White House. The First Lady also called upon the services of the French interior decorator Stéphane Boudin, a former president of the Jansen firm in Paris, about whom she wrote, "When you saw him work, you saw what no American decorator could do. . . . [He gave the rooms] a sense of state, arrival, and grandeur."[7] During this period Mrs Kennedy bought two Zuber *panoramiques*. *Views of North America* were hung in the Diplomatic Reception Room of the White House, while *The War of Independence* graced the private dining room.

This love of wallpaper explains why, even today, many remarkable examples are preserved in historic homes in the United States, not to mention the many the fine pieces found in American public collections.

6. Ruth Lord, *Henry F. Du Pont and Winterthur: A Daughter's Portrait* (New Haven: Yale University Press, 1999), p. 186.
7. *Designing Camelot – The Kennedy White House Restoration* by James Abbot and Elaine Rice. Ed. Van Nostrand Reinhold, ITP, NY 1998.

Les Chasses de Compiègne, two panels of the scenic wallpaper designed by Carle Vernet and wood-block printed by Jacquemart & Bénard in 1815. A complete set was hung c. 1818 in the Kentucky plantation home of Colonel William Rodes for a reception in honor of the Marquis de Lafayette. It is currently in the Historic Governor William Owsley House, listed in the United States' National Register of Historic Places, situated in Lancaster, Kentucky.

LEFT *Beauport-Merriman Papers* Chinese wallpaper, c. 1760. This decor was brought back directly from China to America on the first American ship *Empress of China*. The papers remained intact in a crate until the 1920s when they were installed by the decorator Henry Davis Sleeper. Part of the decor was hung in the ballroom of the Merriman residence in Providence, Rhode Island, and the other part was used by Sleeper at his Beauport summer home in Gloucester, Massachusetts. Peabody Museum, Salem, Massachusetts.

FACING PAGE Chinese wallpaper from the 18th century, bought by Henry Francis Du Pont for his Winterthur residence in 1928. Winterthur Museum, Wilmington, Delaware.

LEFT *F*ragment of an *arabesque* decor designed by Réveillon in 1789. This same paper on a white ground was used in the entrance hall of the Phelps-Hatheway House in Suffield, Connecticut, where four other fine late 18th century Réveillon décors were installed. Musée du Papier Peint, Rixheim (formerly Follot Collection).

FACING PAGE, TOP *Les Jardins Français*, wallpaper designed by Pierre Antoine Mongin and wood-block printed by Zuber in 1822. Installed at Gracie Mansion, residence of the Mayor of New York, by the decorator Albert Hadley in the 1980s and recently renovated by Jamie Drake of Drake Design Associates, New York.

FACING PAGE, BOTTOM *S*cenes from *Vues d'Amérique du Nord*, scenic wallpaper designed by Jean-Julien Deltil and printed by Zuber in 1834. A modified version, including scenes from the American War of Independence, was re-issued in 1852. In 1961 Jacqueline Kennedy hung this paper in the Diplomatic Reception room of the White House. White House Historical Association Collection.

AESTHETIC RENEWAL AND THE ROAD TO MODERN ART

5

Femmes Drapées dans un Paysage Cubiste, designed by René Crevel, printed by the Société Française du Papier Peint, c. 1930. Musée des Arts Décoratifs, Paris.

1. Lesley Hoskins (ed.), *The Papered Wall: History, Pattern, Technique* (New York: Harry N. Abrams, 1994), p. 141.

It is in England that the next aesthetic renewal took place. Following the Great Exhibition of 1851, the English felt bitterly nostalgic for the days when they had dominated the market. As the decorator and manufacturer John Gregory Crace put it in 1849, "To be obliged to cry *peccavi* and at once acknowledge inferiority to our continental neighbor is almost too much for flesh and blood to endure!"[1]

The English rose to the challenge at the international expositions held in London in 1862 and Paris in 1867, and their papers, in contrast with the more illusionist French designs, won many prizes.

A reform movement arose in England to counter the decline in aesthetic design provoked by industrial production methods, with the art critic John Ruskin advocating a return to craftsmanship. Sir Walter Scott popularized medieval romanticism, inspiring the Gothic Revival whose foremost advocate was Augustus Pugin who drew inspiration from medieval fabrics and manuscripts with their heraldic emblems, strong colors, and drawings without perspective. A prolific designer of wallpapers, which he had printed by Crace, he created some for the New Palace of Westminster and the Parliament around 1850, of which *Tudor* is the most well known example. Designed to enrich architecture, his wallpapers were more Gothic than the Gothic structures themselves.

It was Owen Jones who spearheaded the Design Reform movement that rejected the excesses of industrialization and sought inspiration from the past. In his encyclopedic anthology of styles, *The Grammar of Ornament* (1856), he developed a vocabulary of abstract and Islamic-inspired patterns that significantly influenced the prevailing aesthetic.

RIGHT *Wallpaper* designed by Viollet-le-Duc for the 1867 Exposition Universelle in Paris, the manufacturer Isidore Leroy, France. Musée des Arts Décoratifs, Paris.

FACING PAGE *Wallpaper* designed by A.W.N. Pugin for Westminster Palace, London, c. 1850. Victoria and Albert Museum, London.

PAGE 156 *Persian* design, by William Morris, wood-block printed by Jeffrey & Co., London, c. 1875. Victoria and Albert Museum, London.

PAGE 157 *Sunflower* wallpaper, by William Morris, wood-block printed by Jeffrey & Co., London, 1879. Victoria and Albert Museum, London.

William Morris, also nostalgic for the past and particularly fascinated by the Middle Ages, created a circle of artists that included John Ruskin, Aubrey Beardsley, Dante Gabriel Rossetti, and Edward Burne-Jones. In 1861 Morris founded his first workshop, where he wrote poetry and produced manuscripts, textiles, tapestries, stained glass, and wallpaper; his credo was that a craftsman should know how to do everything because all of the arts were interrelated.

In France, meanwhile, Eugène-Emmanuel Viollet-le-Duc was promoting the neo-Gothic movement. Although he is known above all as the restorer of a number of major French buildings, Viollet-le-Duc also taught ornamental composition at the École des Beaux-Arts in Paris, where he encouraged the reinvention of medieval motifs. He clearly inspired a new genre of ornamentalists.

FACING PAGE, LEFT Full height of wall lined with William Morris wallpaper, comprising a frieze, a middle field, and a dado, wood-block printed by Jeffrey & Co., London, c. 1875. Victoria and Albert Museum, London.

FACING PAGE, RIGHT Proposed wallpaper design by Alphonse Mucha, from his *Documents Décoratifs* (1902). Bibliothèque Forney, Paris.

The Aesthetic Movement, which Morris joined, was fashionable between 1870 and 1880. Advocating the idea of art in the home, the "domestic renaissance" promoted by Oscar Wilde, involved a new reorganization of wall space that favored the creation of wallpapers. The flat surface was divided into three parts—dado, filling, and frieze—in order to create more contained and intimate spaces. This new approach underscored the increasing importance of the frieze. Morris produced two-dimensional decorative art, completely ignoring trompe-l'oeil. His ornamentation was inspired by a variety of styles—Renaissance, Venetian, Indian, and Queen Anne—and included countless floral motifs. He also re-launched the old flocking technique imitating velvet or silk developed by the *domino* makers. As of 1864, his many wallpaper designs were printed with wood-blocks by the famous firm of Jeffrey & Co. His papers became enormously popular and were exported all over the world.

Other designers involved in this movement included Edward William Godwin and Christopher Dresser, who tended toward Japanese-inspired wallpapers.

Reform of the decorative arts assumed its full scope with the Arts and Crafts Movement, whose first exhibition in 1888 was seen as a reaction against Queen Victoria's conventional taste. Walter Crane and the architect-decorators Arthur Mackmurdo and Charles Voysey joined Morris. Voysey created more than two hundred designs for wallpaper, mostly produced by the Essex & Co. factory, and became Morris's true successor.

Crane, the first president of the Arts & Crafts Society, along with Mackmurdo, was the leading figure of the new style. Like Morris, Crane felt that a design should remain two-dimensional so that it could be repeated and aligned easily. He designed ceiling papers that were coordinated with wall and frieze papers. His style featured a combination of naturalistic elements, often at the limit of the abstraction of Japanese art. His fluid, synthesizing line was expressed in large, interlacing forms and soft colors. Crane also created wonderful books and wallpapers for children.

The Aesthetic and Arts and Crafts movements had an enormous impact in Europe and America, prefiguring the arrival of art nouveau. The arts were infused with a new spirit—designers wanted to be resolutely modern. The Belle Époque thus invented its own style, though not without criticism from the conservative camp.

In France, Louis Majorelle and Émile Gallé incorporated organic, sensual forms and colors into their designs, drawing their inspiration from a close observation of nature. As Gallé explained, "Our roots are found deep in the woods, at the edge of springs, on mosses."[2] The Belgian Victor Horta invented an entire world of cyclical curves and tendrils, like Alphonse Mucha with his swirling hair, waves, and slender-stemmed flowers inspired by strange, poisonous flora, poppies, and water-lilies. He became the fin-de-siècle artist par excellence of the free-flowing *arabesque*.

Artists and designers of this time sought to create a "total art" that would merge art and life, artist and artisan, as well as house and decoration in order to become one work of art. A unique sense of mural decoration evolved. Art Nouveau wallpapers favored plant and floral motifs, as well as soft colors. Landscape often became the sole theme, with fewer and fewer figures. The frieze, now wider and higher, was no longer hidden by furniture and became essential to structure the decor.

The famous French architect and decorator Hector Guimard displayed striking vitality, shocking people with his construction, in 1895 in Paris, of the Castel Béranger apartment house, at 14 rue La Fontaine. There, he created a "total art" of disquieting baroque inventiveness, where the papers even followed the curvilinear wall paneling. With Guimard, lines no longer existed: "For me, it's not the flower that I like to paint as a decorative element, but the stem."[3] This mural decor created a unified visual realm that included the ornamental ironwork, objects, floors, and furniture. Obviously, this originality was unsettling to the French, and Guimard himself joked about the discomfort of tenants confronted with his wallpapers: "I don't know. . . . It's that paper . . . it has a funny effect on me."[4]

2. Émile Gallé, quoted in Françoise Teynac, Pierre Nolot, and Jean-Denis Vivien, *Le Monde du papier peint* (Paris: Berger-Levrault, 1981), p. 151.
3. Philippe Thiébault, *Guimard, l'Art Nouveau* (Paris: Gallimard, 1992), p. 35.
4. *Ibid.*, p. 37.

ABOVE *Bamboo* wallpaper designed by Edward William Godwin,
printed by Jeffrey & Co., London, 1873. Victoria and Albert Museum, London.

FACING PAGE *Wallpaper*, by Charles Voysey, printed by Essex & Co., London, c. 1880.
Victoria and Albert Museum, London.

ABOVE Walter Crane's *Hey Diddle Diddle* design for a child's room—his great specialty—printed by Jeffrey & Co., London, 1876. Victoria and Albert Museum, London.

FACING PAGE *Iris* wallpaper designed in a Japanese spirit by Walter Crane, printed by Essex & Co., London, c. 1878. Victoria and Albert Museum, London.

PAGE 164 *Pimpernel* wallpaper, by William Morris, block-printed by Jeffrey & Co., London, 1876. Victoria and Albert Museum, London.

PAGE 165 The only known wallpaper executed to a design by Alphonse Mucha, c. 1900. Musée du Papier Peint, Rixheim.

5. *Ibid.*, p. 62.
6. Teynac, Nolet, and Vivien, *Le Monde*, p. 154.
7. *Ibid.*

What the French called *style nouille* (noodle style) prompted sharp criticism. Octave Mirbeau railed that "Nothing is straight anymore … everything turns, twists, jigs, and goes topsy-turvy; everything rolls, winds, unwraps, and suddenly tumbles, with no rime or reason … the furniture looks totally drunk." [5] The novelist Colette was even more blunt when, invited to visit the home of the cabaret star Yvette Guilbert, she declared, "I'd rather be spanked in public than sleep in that puff pastry." [6]

Art nouveau indisputably reached its height at the Exposition Universelle held in Paris in 1900, a mythical year for the Belle Époque, dedicated to the "City of Light," to which people thronged. For this event, the Grand Palais and Petit Palais were built, as were Guimard's famous metro entrances. The national pavilions each adopted very different styles. Everyone who was anyone in the arts in Europe participated. Guimard exhibited the wallpapers he had designed for Castel Béranger. The polemic about art nouveau reached its height, and in the words of the architect Le Corbusier, "in 1900, the fire burst into flames." [7]

Art nouveau was everywhere. Belgium had Victor Horta, Paul Hankar, and Henry van de Velde; in Britain, Charles Rennie Mackintosh was at work in Glasgow; in Germany the Jugenstil movement, highly influenced by Morris, earned renown with the wallpapers of Otto Eckmann, printed by the Engelhardt firm in Mannheim, as well as the more geometrically inclined Hans Christiansen, Peter Behrens, and Richard Riemerschmidt.

168

FACING PAGE *Les Bateaux roses*, by Maurice Denis, 1893.
Musée Départemental du Prieuré, Saint-Germain-en-Laye.

ABOVE Wallpaper with ship and dolphin pattern designed by Christopher Dresser,
printed by Isidore Leroy, France, c. 1902. Musée des Arts Décoratifs, Paris.

LEFT *Flamingo* wallpaper designed in a
Japanese spirit by Otto Eckman for
Engelhard, Mannheim, c. 1898. Deutsches
Tapetenmuseum, Kassel.

FACING PAGE *Beattmuster* wallpaper
designed by Richard Riemerschmidt,
printed by Engelhard, Mannheim, c. 1899-
1900. Deutsches Tapetenmuseum, Kassel.

FACING PAGE *Leipzig* wallpaper designed by Josef Hoffmann for the Wiener Werkstätte, dated 1913–15. Deutsches Tapetenmuseum, Kassel.

ABOVE *Mermaids* wallpaper designed by Koloman Moser, 1901. Fogg Art Museum, Cambridge, Massachusetts.

ABOVE *Viola* wallpaper, by Dagobert Peche, c. 1921. Deutsches Tapetenmuseum, Kassel. The Kassel museum owns a large collection of Peche's papers.

FACING PAGE *Die Rose* wallpaper, by Dagobert Peche, c. 1921. Deutsches Tapetenmuseum, Kassel.

In Germany and Austria the movement tended toward a more pure and simple style. The first Secession in Vienna, launched by Joseph Maria Olbrich and Gustav Klimt in 1897, favored straight lines and flat surfaces. This new rigor and refinement was pursued in the Wiener Werkstätte, the decorative-arts workshops founded in 1903 by Josef Hoffmann. Famous artists such as Koloman Moser and Hoffmann himself designed wallpapers, and Dagobert Peche brought gaiety and lightness, although he constricted the flora to straight lines. The earlier excesses of art nouveau guided certain designers towards greater sobriety. From then on, as the style became more subdued, it started to prefigure art deco.

Paris, from the turn of the twentieth century to the start of World War I, remained a center of dynamic creativity.

The Ballets Russes created a shock in 1909 with their unusual "barbaric" sets and costumes designed by Leon Bakst, launching new fashions in painting, music, decoration, and wallpaper.

In 1910, the furniture designer Émile-Jacques Ruhlmann—who had begun his career as a wallpaper designer—showed his work at the Salon de la Société des Artistes Décorateurs. André Groult, meanwhile, presented his first decorative creations at the Salon d'Automne of that year. By 1911 Groult was himself designing wallpaper as well as issuing other artists' works: Laboureur, who studied lithography under Toulouse-Lautrec and was considered one of the best graphic artists of the day, created *Le Marin* (The Sailor); Barbier modernized Chinese motifs; and Marie Laurencin, a member of the avant-garde Bateau-Lavoir group, painted *Les Singes* (Monkeys) and her famous *Apollinaire*, her lover and mentor, to whom she gave the features of a strange, pointy-headed creature.

Paul Poiret, the great fashion designer and art lover who also adored interior decoration and furnishings, was strongly affected by a trip to Vienna, where he had met Hoffmann and Klimt. Back in Paris, he opened a school of decorative arts, L'Atelier Martine, composed of young women. His *petites Martines* (little Martines) were named after his second granddaughter, who had no artistic training, and were encouraged to express their creativity freely. Poiret maintained close ties to contemporary art circles, including Henri Matisse, André

ABOVE Wallpaper border, French manufacturer, c. 1910–15. Musée des Arts Décoratifs, Paris.

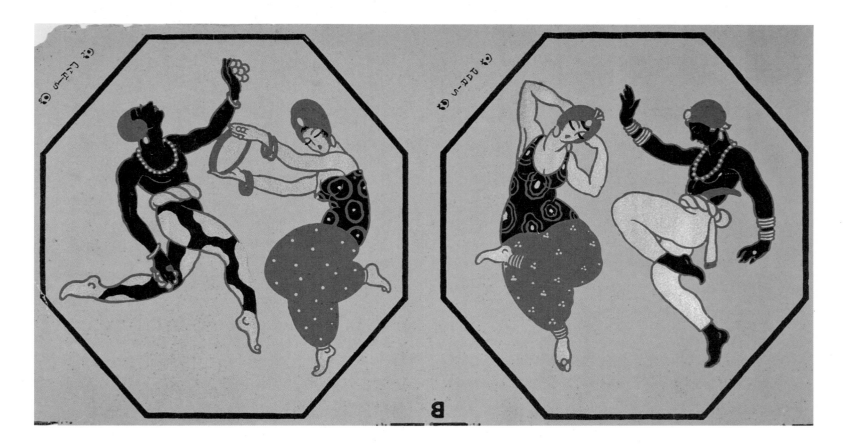

ABOVE *Ballets Russes*, a pair of medallion papers inspired by Diaghilev and Nijinsky for the ballet based on Debussy's *Afternoon of a Faun*, printed by E. M. Gaillard, Paris, c. 1912–15. Deutsches Tapetenmuseum, Kassel, (formerly Bernard Poteau Collection).

ABOVE *Project* for a wallpaper attributed to Suzanne Agron, gouache, France, c. 1925. Carolle Thibaut-Pomerantz Collection.

FACING PAGE *Apollinaire* (or *Isis*) wallpaper designed by Marie Laurencin for André Groult, printed by Alfred Hans & Fils, Paris, 1911. A fine example of Dadaist whimsy. Private collection, Paris. An identical example is in the Bibliothèque Forney, Paris.

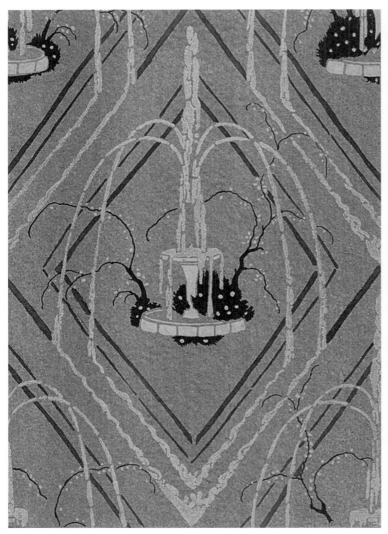

ABOVE, LEFT *Samarkande*, wood-block for a wallpaper designed by Émile Alain Séguy, 1920. Bibliothèque Forney, Paris.

ABOVE, RIGHT *Photo of Paul Poiret's Fountain Dress*. During the art deco period, wallpaper designers often depicted themes of fountains and spurting water.

FACING PAGE *Wallpaper designed by Émile Alain Séguy, printed by Charles Follot, Paris, c. 1920. Bibliothèque Forney, Paris.*

PAGE 184 *Roses* wallpaper designed by Ruhlmann, printed by La Société Française des Papiers, 1925. Bibliothèque Forney, Paris.

PAGE 185 *Eucalyptus* wallpaper, by Atelier Martine, published by Paul Poiret, c. 1912. Bibliothèque Forney, Paris.

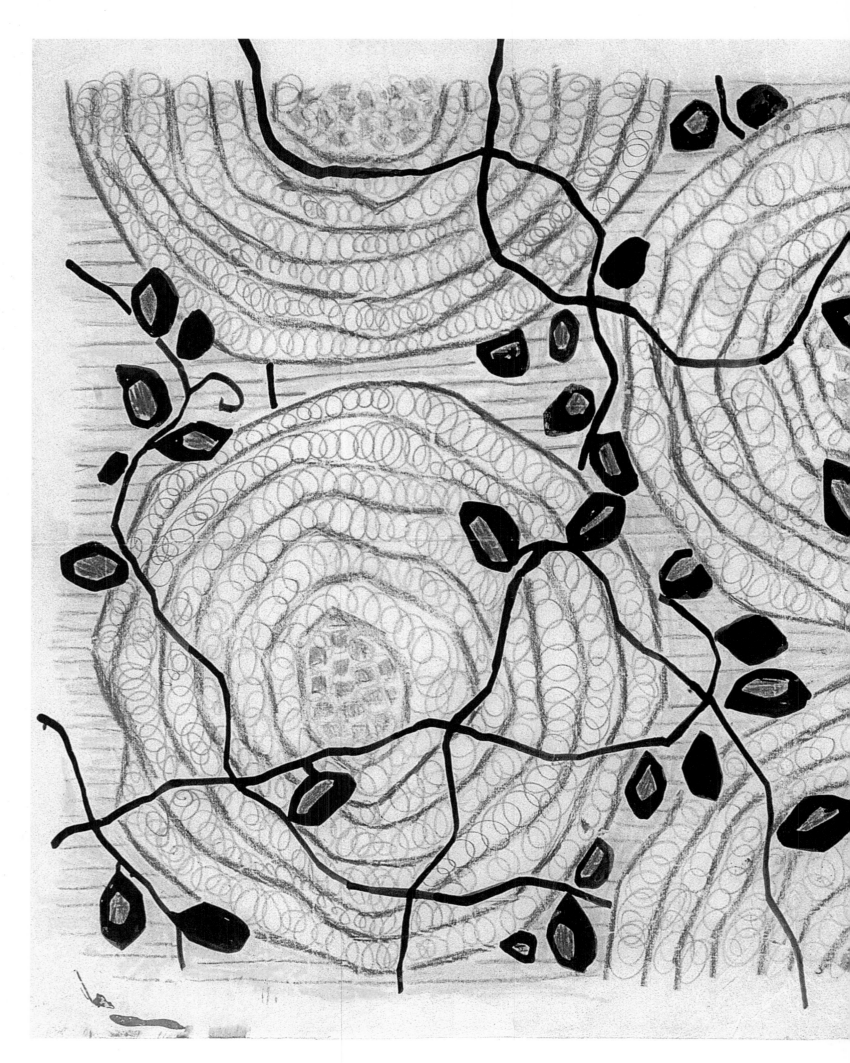

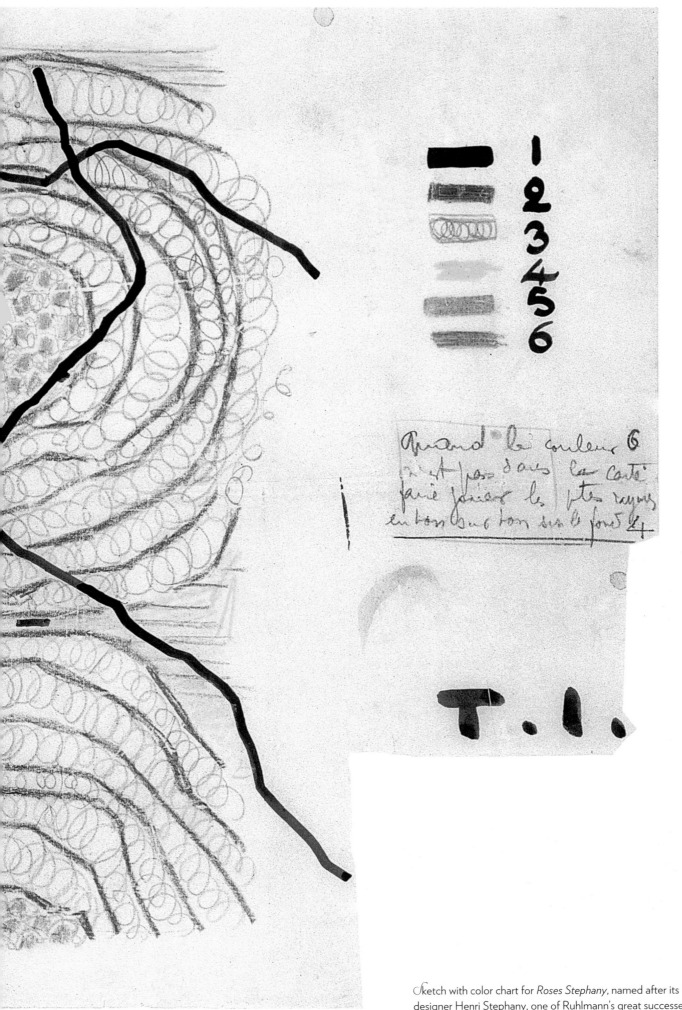

Sketch with color chart for *Roses Stephany*, named after its
designer Henri Stephany, one of Ruhlmann's great successes.

AESTHETIC RENEWAL AND THE ROAD TO MODERN ART 187

LEFT *R*uhlmann wallpaper used in a decor by Jacques Grange. Private collection, London.

FACING PAGE *S*ame wallpaper by Ruhlmann dated 1912, printed by Desfossé & Karth in 1918-23 (marked in the selvedge). Carolle Thibaut-Pomerantz Collection. Other fragments of this paper are conserved at the Metropolitan Museum of Art, New York; Musée des Arts Décoratifs, Paris; and Musée des Années 30, Boulogne-Billancourt.

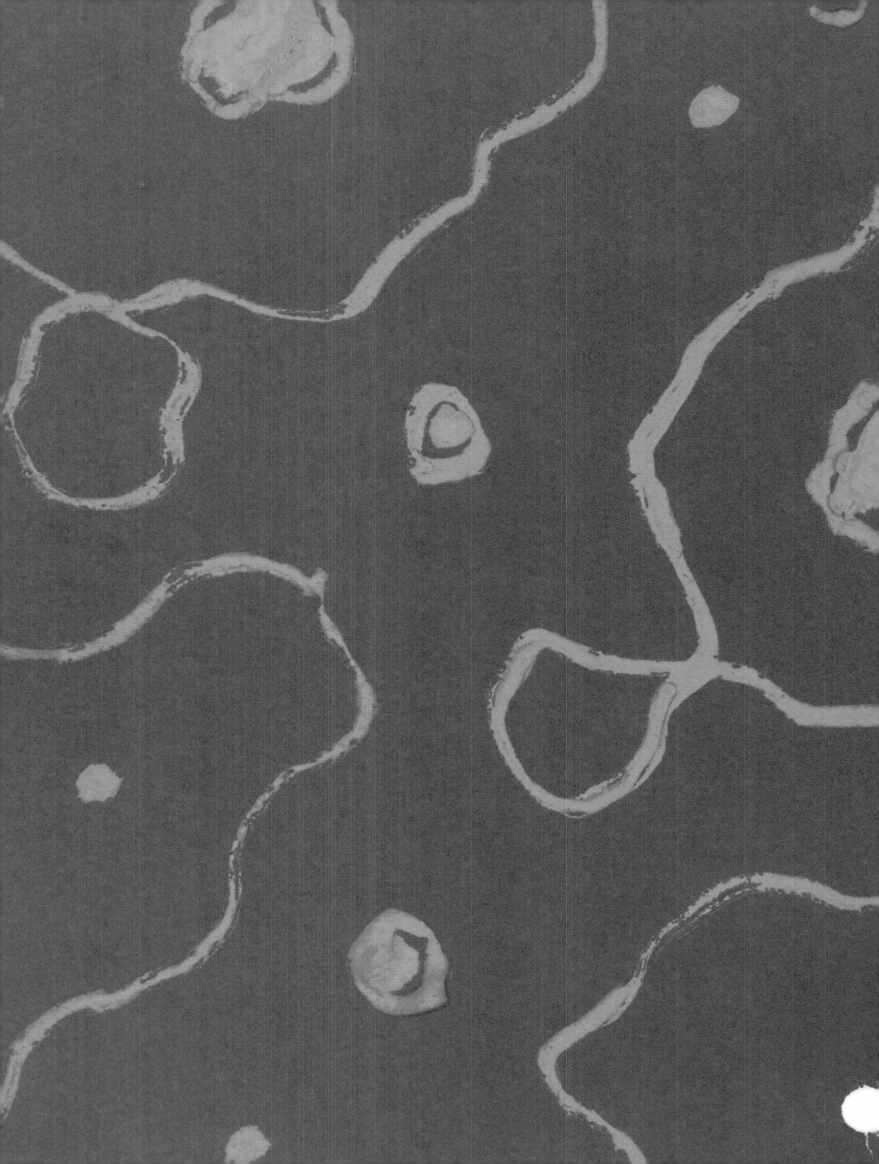

Dunoyer de Segonzac, Kees van Dongen, and Guy-Pierre Fauconnet, and collaborated notably with Raoul Dufy. In 1912, Poiret exhibited the work of L'Atelier Martine at the Salon d'Automne, which featured wallpapers whose designs were often naïve yet showed great freedom and boldness of color and scale.

At that same Salon, a new generation of artists rejected Impressionism, Orientalism, and Art Nouveau. Fauvism and Cubism came to life in painting, along with influences from African Art.

With the relief that accompanied victory after the First World War, the French eagerly embraced the peacetime delights of luxury, eccentricity, and novelty in music, fashion, and furniture. A rare and precious craftsmanship flourished in the Roaring Twenties—the last creative period of a highly refined *savoir faire*. The battle over form was ultimately won by geometry: no trompe-l'oeil, no excessive foliage, just decorative panels on which wallpaper designs conceived as flat surfaces hung comfortably.

Founded by Walter Gropius in 1919, the Bauhaus style which originated from the School of Decorative Arts and the Weimar Fine Arts Academy, had considerable influence all across Europe. "The great work by all, for all"—the Bauhaus philosophy—favored machines and new materials. Wassily Kandinsky headed its painting studio. The Bauhaus sought to eliminate

FACING PAGE *Color sketch for Ruhlmann's Vermicelle, a pattern issued both in wallpaper and fabric.*

RIGHT *Pair of panels, Décor Floral, designed by Stephany for Charles Follot's wallpaper collection, 1929-30. Private collection, New York.*

LEFT *Les Alliés* wallpaper designed by André Mare for La Compagnie des Arts Français, 1919. Private collection, United States. The same wallpaper is conserved in the collection of the Musée des Arts Décoratifs, Paris.

FACING PAGE *Les Mazeraies* designed by Jean Lurçat for Pierre Chareau, exhibited at the 1924 Salon d'Automne. This wallpaper was used in the child's bedroom of the famous Maison de Verre on rue Saint-Guillaume in Paris. It was full of French puns in a playful, Dada spirit: "*j'aime Manon, tu es un clown, un toréador, tu as des chaines, je montre en or*" ("I love Manon, you are a clown, a toreador, you have chains, I a gold watch"). Private collection, New York. A sample of this wallpaper and the original design for the bedroom are in the Musée des Arts Décoratifs, Paris.

PAGES 194-195 Examples of wallpaper from the art deco collection printed by J. Grantil, France, 1928-30. Carolle Thibaut-Pomerantz Collection.

Dessin : 15748-471   Uni vert : 35600-41   Rayure : 35748-461   Bordure encadrement : 55609-471

Rayure : 15737-441

Frise 1 bande : 15624-441

Uni : 35607-45

Bordure : 55601-H441

Frieze, *La Bretagne*, wood-block printed by Charles Henri Geffroy, Paris, 1924, inspired by the painter Mathurin Méheu. Carolle Thibaut-Pomerantz Collection.

8. Charles Follot was a highly cultivated professional who was heir to a major dynasty of wallpaper manufacturers. He modernized the old firm (founded by Philippe Follot in 1859) when he took it over in 1904. The company had first assumed an important role in the industry in 1867, when it had been run by Félix Follot, the first historian of wallpaper, who organized, in 1890, at the behest of the "Committee of the 1868 Contingent," a retrospective celebrating a century of French wallpapers. Felix's son Paul would become one of the interior designers who would show at the 1904 Salon de la Société des Artistes Décorateurs and who would also design wallpapers. The family ran the firm until 1987.
9. Marilyn Oliver Hapgood, *Wallpaper and the Artist from Dürer to Warhol* (New York: Abbeville Press, 1992), p. 164, pl. 154.

the distinction between art and craft, exploiting industrial techniques to produce items in mass quantities according to a new aesthetic.

However it was the Exposition Internationale des Arts Décoratifs et Industriels Modernes (International Exhibition of Decorative and Industrial Arts) held in Paris in 1925 that marked the pinnacle of the art deco style, contributing to the fame of French arts and crafts. All of the greatest designers showed there.

Ruhlmann attracted a good deal of attention with a pavilion called "Le Grand Salon de l'Hôtel du Collectionneur," where he brought together works by a number of artists, among them wall coverings by his associate, Henri Stephany. Ruhlmann masterfully demonstrated the harmony that intimately united interior design and objets d'art. The subtle color relationships reflected his taste for simple yet refined luxury. His very new, yet traditional decor, banished monotony in favor of contrast, giving the pavilion the spirit of the eighteenth-century *folies* in an entirely new tone.

All the best wallpaper manufacturers—Maurice Guin, Le Mardelé, P. A. Dumas, J. Grantil, and Charles-Isidore Leroy—had displays at the 1925 exhibition in Section 14, which was chaired by Charles Follot.[8] In the great tradition of the trade, they employed designers such as Benedictus, Paul Véra, Ruepp, Leleu, and Süe and Mare (who in 1920 founded the Compagnie des Arts Français). The architect Pierre Chareau collaborated with Jean Lurçat, who introduced a fanciful, and very Dadaist, note of madness: "One who loves writes on walls." [9]

The term "ensembliers" came into use. These designers, or artists they commissioned, specialized in creating works designed to produce an all-encompassing decor. Wallpaper was part of the furnishings, thereby contributing to the overall atmosphere. Decorative panels exploded in rich combinations of background papers, large friezes and borders, medallions, and dados—each and every element bold in both color and design. The tones in vogue were smoky gray, purple, violet, yellow and red ochers, shell pink, pale peach, and silver or gold lamés—not far removed from the colors fashionable in textiles at the time.

The art deco period, so rich for wallpaper design, was the last period when high-quality designs by artists were combined with a craft tradition executed in limited editions, often

still printed with wood-blocks despite advances in the use of rotary presses. Thus the special inventiveness of French wallpaper once again enjoyed worldwide recognition.

The obvious success and expansion of this French industry—far ahead of other countries—as seen in the 1925 exhibition, was also reflected in the opening of countless boutiques specialized in decoration which promoted trends, influenced taste, and reinforced the vogue for wallpaper. Thus, Le Mardelé launched his own shop in Paris between the two wars. In 1920, René Gabriel, who trained as a decorator, but referred to himself as a *dominotier*, opened *Les Sansonnets*, a workshop on rue de Solférino (which would give its name to a charming wallpaper). Besson, who opened for business in the 1920s, featured various high-quality artists and manufacturers. The Nobilis boutique, meanwhile, founded by Adolphe Halard on rue Bonaparte in 1928, became famous through the work of the designers Paule Marrot and René Gabriel.

One new development was the applied arts workshops opened by department stores which also produced limited editions of fine wallpapers such as *La Maîtrise* (Mastery) of the Galeries Lafayette in 1921, *Primavera* (Spring) of Le Printemps in 1922, and *Pomone* (Pomona) at Le Bon Marché in 1923.

Several exhibitions demonstrated a continuing interest in wallpaper. Henri Clouzot organized one such show at the Musée Galliera in 1928. In 1933, it was followed by a presentation of a large part of the Follot manufacture's historic collection, organized in conjunction with an exhibition entitled *150e Anniversaire de la Conquête de l'Air – Exposition Historique de l'Aérostation – Rétrospective du Papier Peint* (150th Anniversary of Hot-air Ballooning [...] Retrospective of Wallpapers): the first ascent had occurred on the grounds of the Réveillon wallpaper manufactory. On this occasion public attention was drawn to "the glory of [French] artisans and a truly French decorative art."

Finally, the 1930s saw an increasing sobriety invade the decorative arts, a change already advocated by Le Corbusier in the 1925 exhibition with his "New Spirit" pavilion, which promoted, as Frank Lloyd Wright did in America, what was referred to as a "clinical" style. The color beige would triumph. With his rallying cry, "Cover your walls in whitewash, you will see more clearly into yourselves!", Le Corbusier pointed the way toward a new aesthetic far removed from decorative art.

ABOVE *A* large floral medallion in the bright colors typical of the 1920s, attributed to Charles Henri Geoffroy, France, c. 1925. Carolle Thibaut-Pomerantz Collection. An example of this paper is in the Musée des Arts Décoratifs, Paris.

FACING PAGE *F*ruit-basket pattern of Japanese inspiration, probably designed as an overdoor, wood-block printed and highlighted in silver-leaf by Charles Henri Geffroy, 1925. Carolle Thibaut-Pomerantz Collection. An example is in the collection of the Bibliothèque Forney, Paris.

BACKGROUND *A*vril wallpaper designed by Paule Marrot for the "Collection du Chaud Soleil" printed by Nobilis, 1936. Bibliothèque Forney, Paris.

PAGE 200 *Les Sansonnets* (Starlings), by René Gabriel, wood-block printed by Papiers Peints de France, 1921. Bibliothèque Forney, Paris.

PAGE 201 *Charmilles* (Love Birds) designed by Palyart in 1924 for the Maîtrise, Atelier d'Art of the Galeries Lafayette. Bibliothèque Forney, Paris.

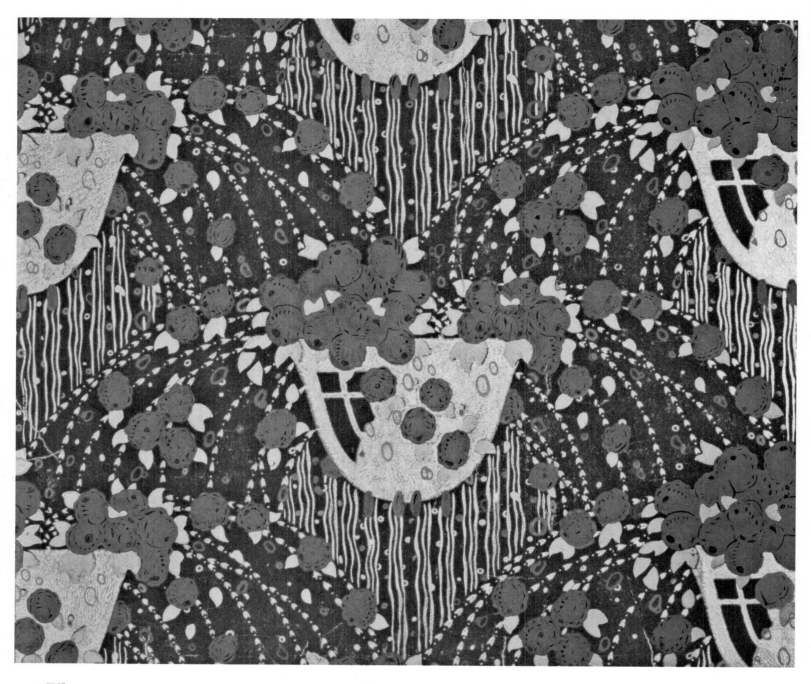

ABOVE Wallpaper by Paul Follot for *Pomone*, Atelier d'art of Bon Marché, Paris, 1925.
Bibliothèque Forney, Paris.

FACING PAGE Wallpaper for *Primavera*, Atelier d'art of Printemps, Paris, 1918–20.
Bibliothèque Forney, Paris.

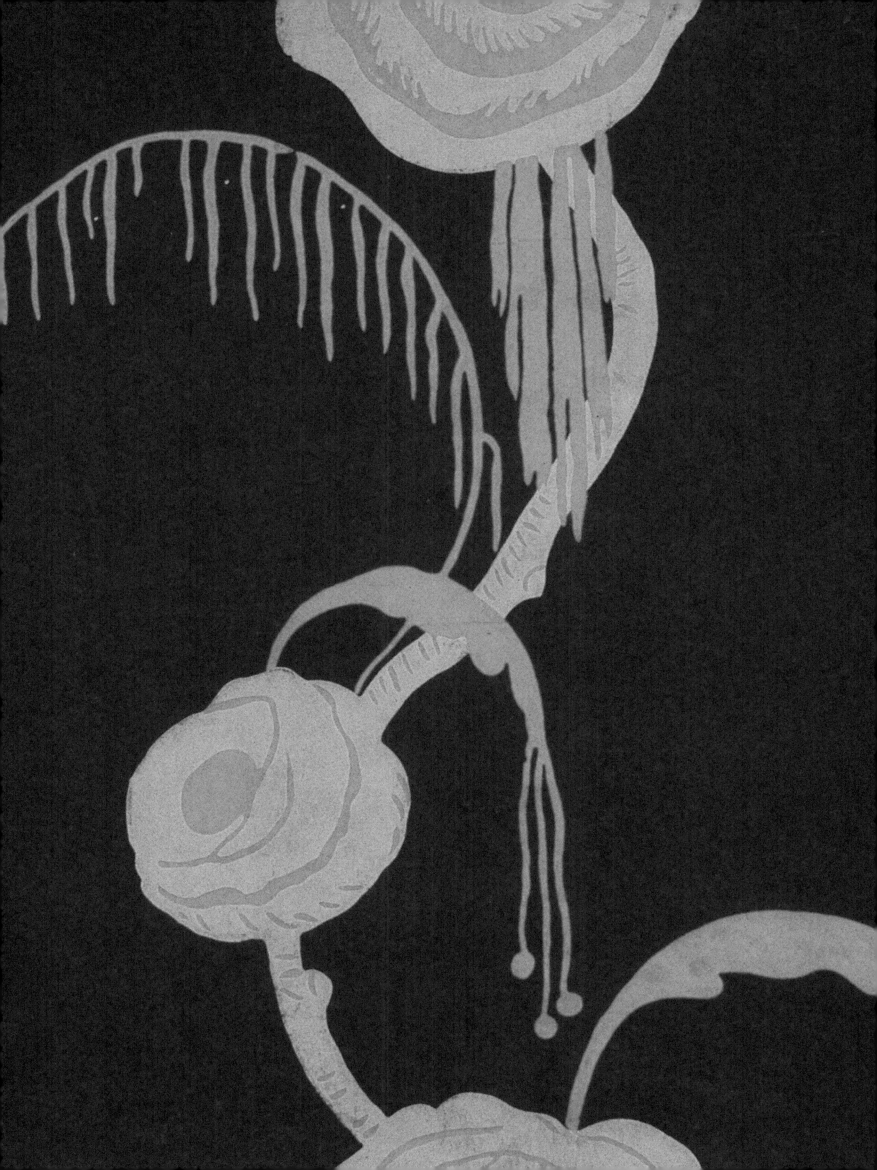

LEFT *Les Perruches* (Parakeets), by René Gabriel, wood-block printed, highlighted in gold leaf, 1915-20. Musée des Arts Décoratifs, Paris.

FACING PAGE *Perroquets* (Parrots) designed by Georges Barbier for André Groult, printed by Alfred Hans, highlighted in gold leaf, Paris, c. 1920. Musée des Arts Décoratifs, Paris.

THE CONTEMPORARY REVOLUTION

6

The shock of World War II provoked an incredible renewal, not only in Europe, where everything had to be rebuilt, but also in the United States, where nothing had been destroyed, and an increasingly avant-garde architecture was developing, notably in New York and Chicago.

America, hungry for novelty, recovered its dynamism and prosperity. People's interests changed radically: lifestyle was easier and became simpler. The arrangement of homes was conceived differently: living and dining rooms were combined, kitchens became more social areas and bathrooms became larger and more attractive.

Wallpaper therefore assumed an entirely different role, with consumers seeking wall coverings that were simultaneously new, cheerful, and practical. Thanks to developments in printing technology such as silk screening and photogravure; the use of synthetic, hygienic, and washable materials such as plastic; and vinyl with its variously matte and glossy surfaces, wallpaper adapted to modern life. Easy to replace, it faithfully reflected a time when fashions and decoration changed at a furious pace, and when people moved homes frequently. The consumer society, driven by the expanding American economy encouraged the production of an infinite selection of items. Movies, Hollywood sets, the Wild West, television, sports, air travel, and space exploration would all influence American lifestyle and be reflected in the decorative patterns on offer.

This new infatuation encouraged wallpaper manufacturers to issue new collections in limited editions and they turned to the old European formula of commissioning works from artists and designers. Tommi Parzinger and especially Ilonka Karasz, who emigrated from Europe and was a great success at the New York World's Fair of 1939, designed papers

Le Poète, by Léonor Fini, printed by Société Française des Papiers Peints, 1948. Musée des Arts Décoratifs, Paris.

with large geometric patterns for Katzenbach & Warren. In 1948 this firm asked Alexander Calder, Henri Matisse, Roberto Matta, and Joan Miró to collaborate on the *Mural Scroll* collection. In 1950 the Schiffer firm in New York turned to Ray Eames, Salvador Dalí, and George Nelson to create Surrealist fabrics which proved so popular that the firm printed matching wallpaper. In reaction to the gloom of the war years, the talented illustrator Saul Steinberg favored a naïve and playful style in bright colors; many of his wallpaper designs were inspired by romantic Paris, as revived by Dior's "New Look" introduced in 1947.

Starting in 1955, Frank Lloyd Wright designed Abstract Geometric wallpapers for Schumacher in neutral or primary colors; these papers were conceived as part of his architecture, not as mere decorative elements. Wright's designs stood out against the wall more than Le Corbusier's cleaner style. The elimination of ornamental motifs provoked, in turn, a revival of interest in the imitation of materials such as leather, tortoise-shell, and wood. This led to an enormously popular novelty, "grass-woven paper" or grass cloth, inspired by the Japanese and Scandinavians.

ABOVE *American Landscape*,
by Ilonka Karasz, printed by Katzenbach
& Warren, New York, 1952. Cooper-Hewitt
National Design Museum, New York.

FACING PAGE *Project* for a wallpaper
design used as the cover of
The New Yorker magazine, 1959.
Carolle Thibaut-Pomerantz Collection.

The "design" concept, of major influence, turned toward an avant-garde style in which space was conceived globally—one single wall became the focal point providing color, life, and sparkle to an entire interior. As of 1950, New York's Museum of Modern Art (MoMA) played a crucial role in these developments by helping to popularize the most innovative, progressive, and indeed provocative art and design. Through its *Good Design* exhibitions, MoMA became a showcase for new accessories, promoting the home furnishing industry. Decoration magazines such as *Better Homes & Gardens* and *House Beautiful* were instrumental in awakening public awareness to the tastes of the day.

America's influence asserted itself in the post-war period. Europe was in ruins. Apartments were hastily and poorly constructed, with small rooms devoid of moldings and cornices. Every surface was flat, hence ideal for wallpaper, which provided a new, easy decoration. Indeed, rampant consumerism was on the rise in Europe, reinforcing interest in wallpaper.

However it was necessary to express the new needs of the time, while also reviving a certain elegance dear to the Old World. Decoration became of prime importance and provoked a veritable rebirth of wallpaper.

ABOVE, TOP *Arbre en Fleur* (Flowering Tree) designed by Henri Matisse, printed by Katzenbach & Warren, New York, 1948. Cooper-Hewitt National Design Museum, New York.

ABOVE, BOTTOM *El Sol*, wallpaper by Joan Miró, printed by Katzenbach & Warren, New York, 1948. Cooper-Hewitt National Design Museum, New York.

FACING PAGE *Splotchy*, wallpaper by Alexander Calder, printed by Laverne Originals, New York, 1949. Rhode Island School of Design, Providence.

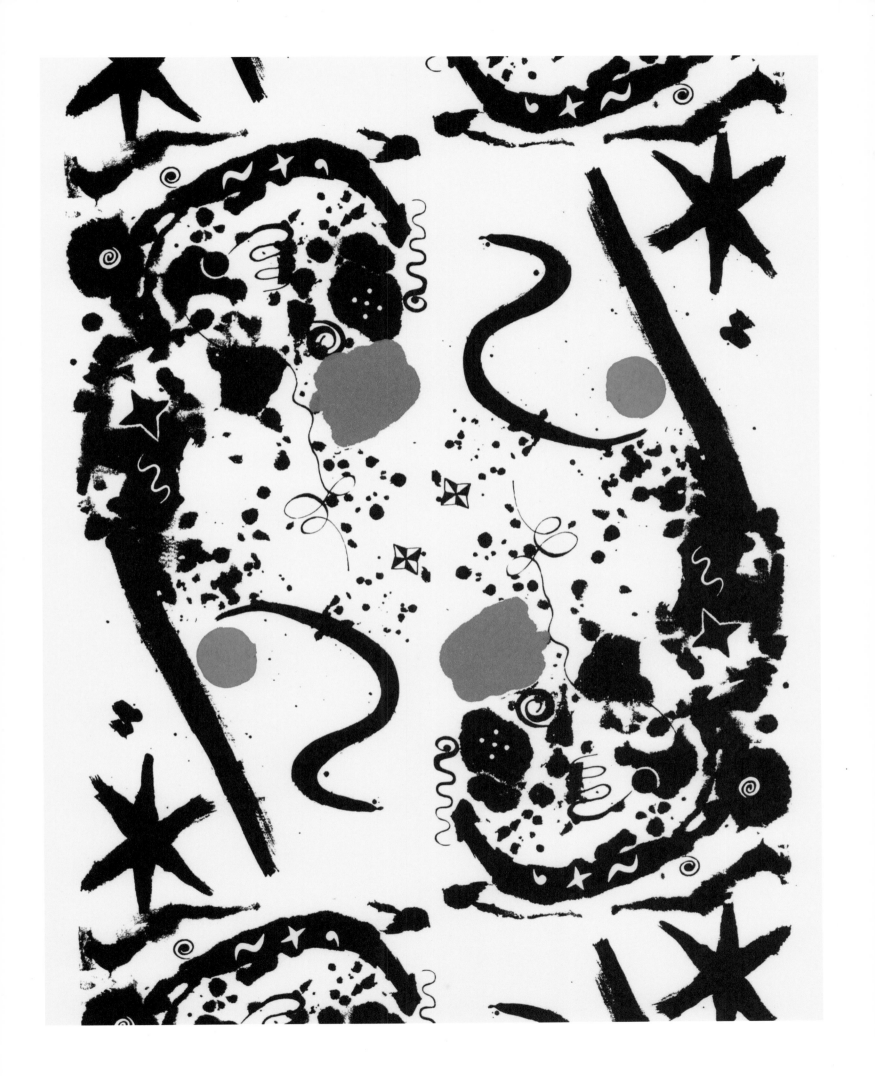

LEFT *Design 704*, by Frank Lloyd Wright for Schumacher, New York, 1954. Schumacher Archives, United States.

BELOW *Mauer* wallpaper designed by Le Corbusier for Salubra, 1959. Forbo-Salubra Collection, Grenzach-Wylen, Germany.

FACING PAGE *Cervantès* wallpaper also known as *Don Quixote and the Golden Age*, designed by Salvador Dalí in 1960, printed by Gebruder Rasch, Germany, 1959. Gebruder Rasch & Co. Collection, Bramsche, Germany.

The exhibition organized in 1953 at the Musée Galliera, *Les Papiers Peints et les Décorateurs du XVIIIᵉ Siècle à nos Jours* (Wallpapers and Decorators from the 18th Century to the Present), recalled the refinements of the past. Decorative firms such as Serge Roche, Ramsay, Jansen, and André Carlhian staged *mises en scène* (settings) with old and new wallpapers. The *panoramique* found favor among decorators, and André Carlhian, specializing in *boiseries* (wood-paneling) and wallpaper decors since 1921, greatly contributed to the revival of this long-neglected, forgotten tradition and made it fashionable again. The firm's famous "red ledger" became a precious catalog of knowledge about scenic *panoramiques*. Introduced to this particular style of mural art by Henri Clouzot and Nancy McClelland, Carlhian soon became a well-known, highly sought-after expert. His two sons, Robert and Michel, took over the firm in 1952, moving it to the Quai d'Orsay, in Paris. Robert Carlhian in particular defended with great conviction and enthusiasm the art of French wallpaper in decoration.[1]

Two major phenomena influenced the wallpaper boom between 1950–80: the rise of decoration boutiques and the emergence of new print-making companies. Indeed, many shops specializing in interior decoration such as Besson, directed at the time by Madame Borgeaud, an amazing figure greatly admired in Parisian circles, presented high-quality wallpaper collections reflecting technical innovations and using the finest talent. Nobilis turned to new designers such as Suzanne Fontan, the "great lady of wallpaper," who revived drapery motifs, trellis-work, and flowers. Barte, a designer-publisher, specialized in metallic papers, while *La Boutique Américaine*, opened in Paris in 1967, hired the American designer Billy Manzon to present his *Mylar* collection. *Les Dominotiers* opened in 1972, offering a wide selection of top-quality manufacturers. Jean Vigne worked with the photographer Jean-Louis Seigner to produce the famous *Apollo* wallpaper based on NASA photographs.

Major manufacturers collaborated with designers and joined up with makers working in a more traditional manner. For example, André Mauny, originally a prestigious decorator, purchased old printing plates from the *ensembliers* (designers) Robert Caillard and André Groult. Mauny established himself in Paris at 25bis, rue Franklin in the handsome office originally built in 1902 by the architect Auguste Perret. In this showroom-workshop, from 1937 to 1987, he presented papers reproduced from old designs in the great craft tradition, while also creating contemporary decorative decors.

Starting in 1947 and continuing through the 1950s, Paule Leleu, the daughter of the decorator and furniture designer Jules Leleu, produced countless wallpapers that were printed by Follot. The Leleu firm also created beautiful papers for the lavish celebrations held in Persepolis in Iran in 1971 marking the 2,500th anniversary of the Iranian monarchy. Zofia Rostad, who got her start with Paule Marrot, designed numerous patterns and in 1978 signed a wallpaper line for the ESSEF firm. The Belgian Jean-Michel Folon, famous for his little stylized figures that evoke modern *angst* and anonymity in crowds (*foule* in French), devised a wallpaper called *Foultitude* (1969). On his return from the United States, Salvador Dalí produced a paper called *Don Quixote*, also known as *L'Age d'Or* (The Golden Age, 1960).

In Great Britain, manufacturers continued to prefer floral patterns and chintz and drew from their traditional heritage. The stylist Laura Ashley began in the 1950s to market her floral prints successfully in her boutiques throughout the world. At the same time, the designer Lucienne Day created some highly inventive papers inspired by artists such as Miró, Klee, and Calder. Since then, the finest representatives of the "haute couture" of British wallpaper include the Sanderson firm, who has exclusive rights to William Morris's designs, Cole & Son, suppliers to Her Majesty the Queen, Designer's Guild, and Osborne & Little.

ABOVE *Paris Opera*, wallpaper designed by Saul Steinberg, printed by Greeff Fabrics, New York, 1950. Cooper-Hewitt National Design Museum, New York.

FACING PAGE, LEFT *Foultitude* (Crowdedness), wallpaper designed by Jean-Michel Folon, printed by Zuber, 1969. Musée des Arts Décoratifs, Paris.

FACING PAGE, RIGHT *Arc-en-ciel* (Rainbow) wallpaper designed by Zofia Rostad for one of her signed collections, manufactured by Essef Decors, France. Musée du Papier Peint, Rixheim.

1. I am grateful to Robert Carlhian for his support and encouragement of my defense of historic wallpapers.

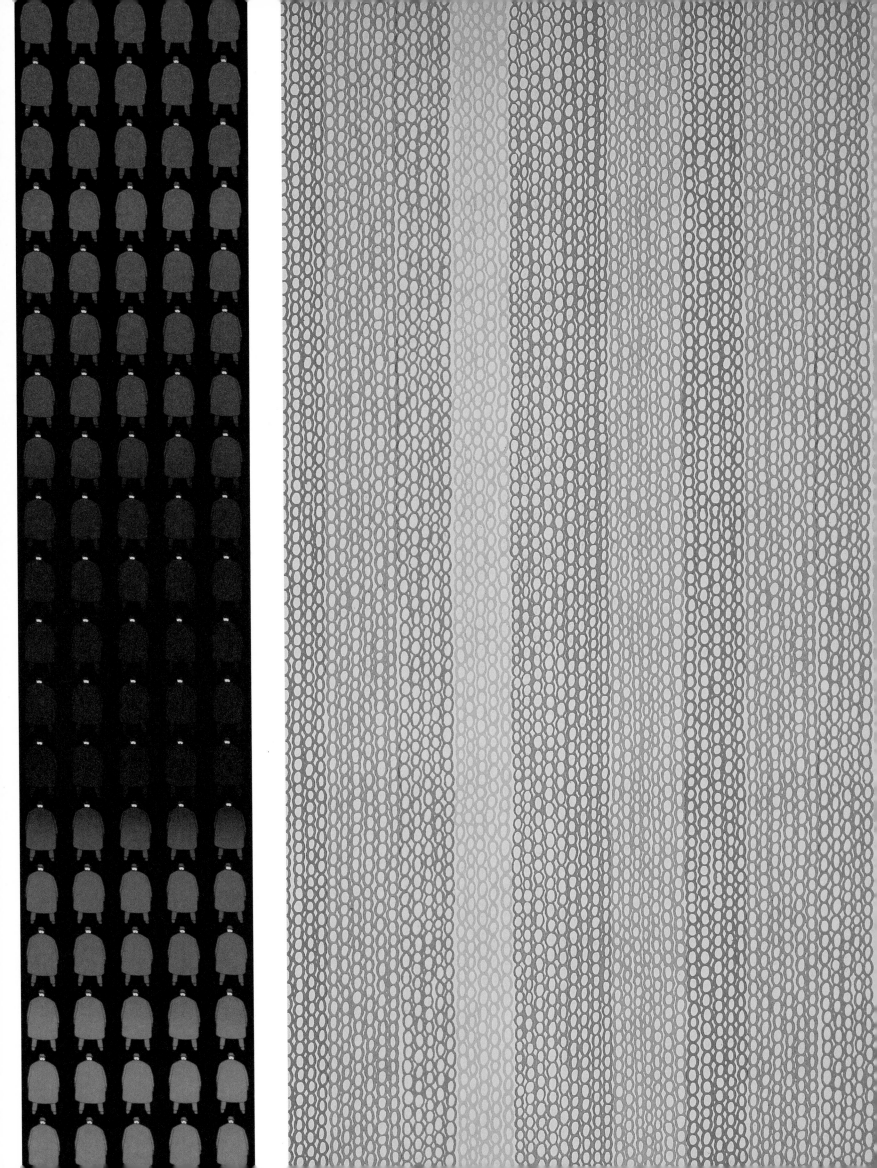

216

ABOVE *Mignonne, Voici l'Avril* (Sweet, April Is Here) wallpaper designed by Suzanne Fontan for Nobilis, 1945. Bibliothèque Forney, Paris.

RIGHT *À Cœur Perdu* ("At Lost Heart" [sic]) wallpaper designed by Charles Portel for Nobilis, c. 1945. Carolle Thibaut-Pomerantz Collection.

FACING PAGE *Vues de Paris* (Views of Paris), a panel from a pair of wallpapers block-printed in grisaille by the manufacturer Mauperny, Paris, 1946–47. Private collection, United States.

PAGE 218 *Prisma* wallpaper by Lucienne Day, one of the best known post-war designers in England; this pattern was part of the Rasch Artist Collection done in the 1950s. Gebruder Rasch & Co. Collection, Bramsche, Germany.

PAGE 219 *Studie* (Study) wallpaper by Margaret Hildebrand, a German designer of the 1950s; this paper was in the Rasch Artist Collection in those years. Gebruder Rasch & Co. Collection, Bramsche, Germany.

FACING PAGE *Compendium* wallpaper designed by Ulf Moritz for *X-Art Walls Collection of Contemporary Artists' Designs*, 1972. Marburger Tapetenfabrik Collection, Kirchain, Germany.

During this period, wallpaper pursued its pas-de-deux between design and contemporary art. In the 1960s, Pop artists sought to narrow the gap between art and commerce, as was demonstrated by Andy Warhol who made a major mark with his *Cow, Mao,* and *Self-Portrait* papers, exhibited at the Leo Castelli Gallery in New York. Repeat patterns delighted Warhol, who reproduced both figures and objects in his artworks, in multiple repetitions, just like wallpaper. The mood of the day was graphic and dynamic—"flower power" favored bright colors, and wallpaper was a perfect medium and means of expression.

In Germany, the Marburg firm commissioned a limited edition in 1972 called the *X-Art Walls Collection of Contemporary Artists' Designs*. This series featured eight artists: Otmar Alt, Getulio Alviani, Werner Berges, Allen Jones, Peter Philips, Paul Wunderlich, Ulf Moritz, Jean Tinguely, and Niki de Saint-Phalle, whose *Nanas* burst with color. In 1974 Marburg launched a "second generation" of papers printed in photogravure with textured effects, reflecting the influence of disco culture. Psychedelic patterns in contrasting colors covered walls, their effects changing as the lighting shifted.

In the 1980s, wallpaper tended to imitate the texture of paint, with a predominance of soft colors, while in the following decade it was Minimalist art that influenced the character of wall coverings.

In 1992, Rasch, another famous German wallpaper manufacturer, issued a line called *Zeitwande* (Wall of Time), developed in collaboration with five European artists including Ettore Sottsass, Borek Sipek, Alessandro Mendini, and George Sowden. The Rasch firm has cultivated a long tradition of collaboration between art and industry, having begun in the 1930s by creating the *Weiner Kunstler-Tapeten* (Viennese Wallcovering Workshop) under the supervision of Josef Hoffmann. In the 1950s, it produced a collection of papers with Lucienne Day and Margaret Hildebrand.

Ultimately, there was a need for a lifestyle magazine with an original concept to report on the continual expansion of wallpapers: that was one of the ideas behind the design magazine *Wallpaper,* launched in England in 1996. Aimed at an affluent, fashion-conscious readership, *Wallpaper* continues to serve as an advocate of modernism and the latest trends.

The exhibition entitled *On the Wall,* jointly organized by the Rhode Island School of Design Museum and the Fabric Workshop and Museum of Philadelphia in 2003, sought to present the creative context governing wallpaper since the 1990s. Within the framework of this show, a selection of thirty-nine contemporary artists demonstrated how to reinvent an original art form. Some used wallpaper as the principal support, while others incorporated it into their work; others used traditional methods of printing, silk screening, or painting, while still others turned to more modern techniques and materials, such as photoengraving, digital imagery, or projection. All of these artists explored the very essence of wallpaper: the principle of repetition as an ornamental device and the concept of wall surface in relation to space and architecture. Whether the approach was surrealistic or conceptual, or took the form of provocative installations focused on contemporary subjects (exemplified by Virgil Marti's *Bullies,* or works by Francesco Simeti, Brian Chippendale, Adam Cvijanovic, and others) they forged a mode of artistic expression that gave new meaning to the imagery and nature of wallpaper. Pieces by Andy Warhol, Roy Lichtenstein (*Interior with Blue Floor*), William Wegman, John Baldessari (*Potato/Lightbulb-blue*), Robert Gober (*Hanging Man, Sleeping Man*), and Do Ho Suh (*Who Am We*) were at the heart of this profusion of art works.

Hardly new, artists' interest in wallpaper as a form of expression, as we have seen, has been explored throughout different periods. Some have produced designs specifically for wallpaper while others have incorporated wallpaper fragments into their own compositions and collages.

ABOVE Wallpaper designed by Otmar Alt for *X-Art Walls Collection of Contemporary Artists' Designs*, 1972. Marburger Tapetenfabrik Collection, Kirchain, Germany.

FACING PAGE *Nana* wallpaper designed by Niki de Saint-Phalle for *X-Art Walls Collection of Contemporary Artists' Designs*, 1972. Marburger Tapetenfabrik Collection, Kirchain, Germany.

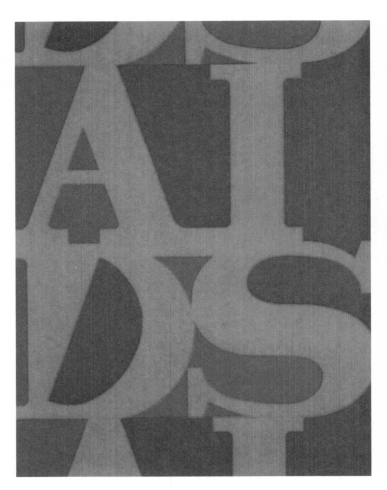

Several recent exhibitions have focused on this interest. In 2004 the Cooper-Hewitt National Design Museum in New York showed its collection of wallpapers executed by renowned artists such as Miró, Calder, Matisse, and Matta. Two years later, the Museum of Modern Art organized *Eye on Europe: Prints, Books & Multiples, 1960 to Now*, which featured *Pharmacy Wallpaper,* a major work by Damien Hirst. The French artist Claude Closky has also designed wallpapers, including a series for the administrative offices of the Pompidou Center in Paris.[2]

A new generation is now producing limited-edition wallpapers using new technologies—digital equipment, photographic enlargement, screen-printing, experiments with textures (non-woven, relief, stickers). Walls come alive with an infinite variety of compositions, or with assemblages of repeated or related images, like in a puzzle, creating a new kind of fresco. Trompe-l'oeil effects, long out of fashion, are coming back, but with a distinctly modern tone. A conventional approach to wall coverings is no longer acceptable—a new type of mural decor is required, between art and design, that reflects the connection to the environment. Acquiring a new dimension and personality, wallpaper is transformed, and gives way to custom-made *mise en scène* according to the taste and fancy of the individual.

In this trend, the sticker is the latest ornamental craze—to be placed wherever one chooses. The LZC trio has produced a *Jardin Autocollant* (Sticker Garden) with motifs of leaves, flowers, and stems that can be arranged anywhere on plain white wallpaper. On the British scene, the avant-garde designer Tracy Kendall has composed a wide variety of papers, some with little fanciful elements in relief, others with more sober floral patterns against black and white grounds, or blending into reworked photos images of stacked plates or magazines. Meanwhile, the designer Deborah Bowness enjoys using photos to reconstitute the old

TOP *Luna*, by Alessandro Mendini, limited-edition wallpaper in the *Zeitwande* collection (Wall of Time), issued by Rasch in 1992 and exhibited at the Deutsches Tapetenmuseum, Kassel. Rasch GmbH & Co. Tapentenfabrik Collection, Germany.

BOTTOM, LEFT *Zed*, by Borek Sipek, limited-edition wallpaper in the *Zeitwande* collection, issued by Rasch in 1992 and exhibited at the Deutsches Tapetenmuseum, Kassel. Rasch GmbH & Co. Tapentenfabrik Collection, Germany.

BOTTOM, RIGHT *Arabia Felix*, by Ettore Sottsass, limited-edition wallpaper in the *Zeitwande* collection, issued by Rasch in 1992 and exhibited at the Deutsches Tapetenmuseum, Kassel. Rasch GmbH & Co. Tapentenfabrik Collection, Germany.

FACING PAGE *Mao* wallpaper by Andy Warhol, part of the *On the Wall—Contemporary Wallpaper* exhibition held at the Museum of Art, Rhode Island School of Design, Providence, and the Fabric Workshop and Museum, Philadelphia, in 2003. Andy Warhol Museum, Pittsburgh.

ABOVE *Interior with Blue Floor* wallpaper by Roy Lichtenstein, 1992, *On the Wall—Contemporary Wallpaper* exhibition held at the Museum of Art, Rhode Island School of Design, Providence, and the Fabric Workshop and Museum, Philadelphia, in 2003. Rhode Island School of Design Museum, Providence.

ABOVE *Butterfly Paper*, designed by Rob Wynne and exhibited at the Holly Solomon Gallery, New York, in 1996. JGM Galerie, Paris.

RIGHT *Éventail* (Fan) wallpaper from an album designed by Karl Lagerfeld, printed by AS Creation, c. 1990. Musée des Arts Décoratifs, Paris.

FACING PAGE *Who Am We?* wallpaper by the Korean artist Do-Ho Suh, 2000. Courtesy of Lehmann Maupin Gallery Collection, New York.

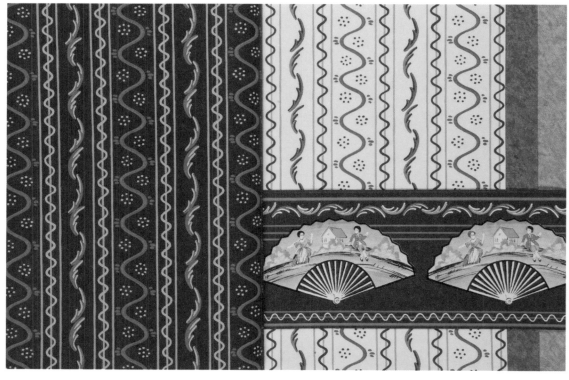

tradition of trompe-l'oeil wallpaper, as reflected in the library she designed for Christian Lacroix's decoration of the Hôtel du Petit Moulin in Paris. In the United States, Wallpaper Lab, a firm founded in 2006, publishes limited-edition papers by fifteen conceptual artists who collaborate to translate their studio works into wall panels or stickers, placing wallpaper design at the heart of their aesthetic reflection. Among them are Richard Kalina, who uses traditional decorative motifs such as flowers to explore concepts of repetition, symmetry, and the relationships of colors confronted to black-and-white; Phoebe Washburn, who composes a montage of a trompe-l'oeil mural of *faux* wood; and Miyeon Lee, who subordinates the colored surfaces of wallpaper to the surrounding architecture.

Today, one must above all distinguish industrial mass-production from work by designers and craftsmen-manufacturers who use the medium of wallpaper to explore other means of artistic expression. Thus, these artists or designers use wallpaper to turn a wall into a totally new work of art.

CONCLUSION

Wallpaper earned its noble reputation—its *lettres de noblesse*—in the late eighteenth century, reaching a level of perfection that made it a symbol of refinement and excellence in the French decorative arts. Originally, paper's relatively inexpensive price compared to other materials was of prime importance in its choice. But as soon as wallpaper transcended mere imitation and developed its own originality and characteristics, it took this new mural art to another level—that of the finest engraving.

The scale and ambition of these decors, the complexity of composition, the quality of printing, and the subtlety of palette and wealth of color all turned wallpaper into an art in its own right—placing it in the heart of decorative arts—and leaving its mark on the history of interior decoration.

Contemporary interior decorators endowed with expertise, culture, sensibility, and imagination are able to adapt these old papers by marrying them to other styles—patterns and features of the eighteenth and nineteenth centuries can go perfectly well with modern furnishings, creating a play of space, color, materials, and periods that can result in surprising and inventive decors.

Art amateurs with eclectic tastes are able to appreciate the beauty and particular interest of this art form and combine it with other collectibles.

The press, ever in search of new trends, has already taken an interest in wallpaper, realizing that there is a story to tell. Through its innumerable illustrated articles, it has helped open the eyes of the public and sparked its interest.

Vintage wallpapers are neither old-fashioned nor fixed in time, they can be adapted to all kinds of styles and appear completely up-to-date.

Large walls are not necessarily needed to present them: as soon as a panel is hung in a small or narrow room, it creates an illusion of depth and expands the sense of space. And if a room lacks luminosity, these papers introduce light.

Of course, it is still possible to use a full decor or complete scenic *panoramique* to create a total ambience, as was done in the past, but it is not always necessary to show it in continuity and to cover all the walls. On the contrary, they can be separated into individual scenes. One or several panels of a set, or a fragment of a decor mounted on a stretcher, can easily find its place, much like an engraving, a painting, or a Japanese screen.

Wallpaper, whether it is historic or contemporary, should therefore not be treated as simple rolls to cover walls, but rather as an object that can be hung, moved, or adapted, using the current expression, "on the wall, off the wall."

Once it is perceived as an art object, wallpaper takes on an entirely new role and dimension. In dialogue with other decorative elements, it becomes a new type of mural design. This is when wallpaper acquires new impact: it becomes the pivot or point of departure of the decoration of an interior, giving it particular originality.

One crucial issue remains. An old master painting represents an original act of individual creativity, whereas wallpaper is an art that calls upon the talents of several craftsmen.

Period papers or contemporary creations are produced in limited editions, somewhat like designer furniture and objets d'art. Does the fact that a piece is not unique mean that it embodies no creativity? Is there any point in maintaining a distinction between the "fine" and the "minor" arts? Such academic terminology is surely out of date. Should a silver bowl

Tribute to Wallpaper, patchwork decor in the home of Signor Buongiorno in London, designed by Laura Sartori Rimini and Roberto Peregalli, successor of the Mongiardino interior design firm, Milan, Italy, 2000.

FACING PAGE *P*anel of a French
Art deco wallpaper, c. 1925, presented
with an armchair by Mathias Bengtsson:
Slice Aluminium Chair, 2000. Decor
by Juan Montoya, Paris.

ABOVE, LEFT *A*rt deco Triptych by J. Grantil,
France, 1928–30, in a contemporary
decor created by Jamie Drake, New York.

ABOVE, RIGHT *P*anel from a large frieze
attributed to Dufour, France, c. 1820,
presented with an armchair *Suite Ingénue*
designed by Sylvain Dubuisson for Mobilier
National, édition Creative Agents, 2006.

by Thomas Germain, a Flemish tapestry, an armchair by Jacob, or a Han or Tang statue be considered a "minor" artwork just because it was created by a craftsman or because it was not produced as a unique piece?

It makes more sense to discount this artificial distinction and instead to recognize that there are major works and minor works within every genre.

This approach, more pertinent to art objects, clearly includes fine creative wallpaper: its bright, lively colors lend magic to an interior, and its patterns and figures, whether flat or in relief, evoke an atmosphere with precision, and can also enlarge a space.

It is not surprising then, that ever since the eighteenth century, the art of wallpaper has influenced fashion, and that interest in the medium, heightened by the infinite variety of decors, continues to grow. Today, wallpaper creations introduce a new spirit, surrealistic or conceptual, sometimes playful and often unique. There is something to suit everyone's taste.

Wallpaper creates an ambience, rebuilds the decor of private little theaters, and breaks down barriers between styles. It plays with and lends itself to baroque-like or extravagant genres—kitsch, picturesque, even quirky art, without abandoning the lessons of the past.

A veritable objet d'art due to the manner in which it is conceived and produced, easy to use and perfectly adapted to our constantly changing world, wallpaper has become much more than an art of fine engraving: it is a means of expressing individual personality in private spaces.

It would appear that wallpaper is once again in the spirit of the time. The importance given to personal homes, the taste for interior decoration and its renewed remodeling take on an increasing role in today's lifestyle: wallpaper, all on its own, brings life and color, and as Paul Valéry so aptly put it, makes "the walls sing".

Scenes from the *panoramique* called *Fêtes Grecques* or *Jeux Olympiques*, by Dufour, France, 1818, presented in a modern decor by Orlando Diaz-Azcuy, San Francisco.

BIBLIOGRAPHY

WORKS IN ENGLISH

ENTWISLE, E.A., *The Book of Wallpaper. A History and an Appreciation*, London, Arthur Barker, 1954.

GORDON-CLARK, Jane, *Wallpaper in Decoration*, New York, Watson-Guptill Publications, 2001.

GREYSMITH, Brenda, *Wallpaper*, London, Cassell & Collier Macmillan Publishers, 1976.

HAPGOOD, Marilyn Oliver, *Wallpaper and the Arts from Dürer to Warhol*, New York, Abbeville Press, 1992.

HOSKINS, Lesley, *The Paper Wall – The History, Patterns and Technique of Wallpaper*, London, Thames and Hudson, 2nd edition, 2005.

KATZENBACH, Lois and William, *The Practical Book of American Wallpaper*, Philadelphia and New York, J.B. Lippincott Company, 1951.

LENCEK, Lena, and BOSKER, Gideon, *Off the Wall. Wonderful Wall Coverings of the Twentieth Century*, San Francisco, Chronicle Books, 2004.

LYNN, Catherine, *Wallpaper in America, from the Seventeenth Century to World War 1*, Barra Foundation, Cooper-Hewitt National Design Museum, W.W. Norton & Company, Inc. New York, 1980.

McCLELLAND, Nancy, *Historic Wallpapers, from their Inception to the Introduction of Machinery*, Philadelphia, J.B. Lippincott Company, 1924.

NOUVEL-KAMMERER, Odile (ed.), *French Scenic Wallpaper*, Musée des Arts décoratifs, Paris, Flammarion, 2000.

NYLANDER, Richard C., *Wallpaper for Historic Buildings*, Washington, The Preservation Press, 2nd edition, 1992.

NYLANDER, Richard C., REDMOND, Elizabeth, and SANDER, Penny J., *Wallpaper in New England*, Boston, Society for the Preservation of New England Antiquities, 2nd edition, 1986.

OMAN, Charles, and HAMILTON, Jean, *Wallpapers, an International History and Illustrated Survey*, New York, Harry N. Abrams Inc., 1982.

SANBORN, Kate, *Old Time Wallpapers*, Greenwich, The Literary Collector Press, 1905.

SAUNDERS, Gill, *Wallpaper in Interior Decoration*, London, V. & A. Publications, 2002.

TANNENBAUM, Judith, and BOULTON-STOUD, Marion, *On the Wall Contemporary Wallpaper*, Philadelphia, Museum of Art, Rhode Island School of Design, 2003.

WHATELET, Alice, *Modern Wallpaper & Wallcovering. Introduction Color, Pattern & Texture into your Living Space*, New York, Universe Publishing, 2002.

WORKS IN FRENCH

BRUIGNAC DE, Véronique, *Arts et techniques : le papier peint*, Paris, Massin, 1995.

BRUIGNAC-LaHOUGUE DE, Véronique, *Art et artistes du papier peint en France*, Paris Gourcuff Gradenigo & Les Arts Décoratifs, 2007.

CLOUZOT, Henri, *Papiers peints et tentures modernes (toiles et cretonnes imprimées)*, Paris, Ch. Massin et Cie Éditeur, 1928.

CLOUZOT, Henri, *Tableaux-tentures de Dufour et Leroy*, Paris, Librairie des Arts décoratifs, A. Calavas éditeur, 1930.

CLOUZOT, Henri, and Follot, Charles, *Histoire du papier peint en France du XVIIᵉ au XIXᵉ siècle*, Paris, Éditions d'art Charles Moreau, 1935.

FIGUIER, Louis, *Une histoire du papier peint, extraits de description des principales industries modernes* [1875], Ouvèze-sur-Sorgues, Trait pour Trait, 1995.

GUSMAN, Pierre, *Panneaux décoratifs et tentures murales du XVIIIᵉ siècle et du commencement du XIXᵉ siècle*, Paris, Ch. Massin Éditeur, 1900.

JACQUÉ, Bernard, and NOUVEL-KAMMERER, Odile, *Le Papier Peint, Décor d'illusion*, Barembach, Éditions Jean-Pierre Gyss, 1987; reprinted in 1989.

TEYNAC, Françoise, NOLOT, Pierre, and VIVIEN, Jean-Denis, *Le Monde du papier peint*, Paris, Berger-Levrault, 1981.

VELUT, Christine, *Décors de papiers – Production, commerce et usage des papiers peints à Paris, 1750-1820*, Paris, Monum, Éditions du Patrimoine, 2005.

Espace d'Art, Art d'Espace, Des intérieurs comme autant d'œuvres d'art – découverts dans les palais, châteaux et monastères d'Allemagne, official guide of the Châteaux de Bade-Wurtemberg, Bavaria, Berlin-Brandebourg, Hesse, Mecklembourg-Poméranie- Antérieure, Rhénanie-Palatinat, Saxe, Saxe-Anhalt, Thuringe. Regensburg, Schnell – Steiner, 2005

EXHIBITION CATALOGS IN ENGLISH

KOSUDA-WARNER, Joanne, and JOHNSON, Elizabeth, *Landscape Wallcovering*, London, Scala Publishers, 2001.

WEBB, Vivienne, *Les Sauvages de la mer Pacifique*, Art Gallery of New South Wales – National Gallery of Australia, Perth, 2000.

A Decorative Art. 19th Century Wallpapers in the Whitworth Gallery, 4 October–21 December 1985, Whitworth Art Gallery, Manchester, 1985.

Kitsch to Le Corbusier, Wallpaper from the 1950's, Cooper-Hewitt National Design Museum – Smithsonian Institution, New York, 1995.

EXHIBITION CATALOGS IN FRENCH

BIERI, Helen, and JACQUÉ, Bernard, *Papiers peints Art nouveau*, Musée du Papier peint, Rixheim, Fondation Neumann, Milan, Skira, 1997.

BRUIGNAC DE, Véronique (ed.), *Une aventure du papier peint – La collection Mauny*, Paris, Bibliothèque Forney, 21 June–21 September 1997, Nantes, Éditions du Conseil général de Loire-Atlantique, 1997.

JACQUÉ, Bernard, *Papiers peints et Révolution*, Rixheim, Musée du Papier peint, 1989.

JACQUÉ, Bernard, *Les Papiers peints en irisé*, June 2004–2005, Rixheim, Musée du Papier peint, 2005.

JACQUÉ, Bernard, *Brésil panoramique – Papiers peints du XIXᵉ siècle*, Bibliothèque Marmottan, Boulogne-Billancourt, Saint-Remy-en-l'Eau, Éditions Monelle Hayot, 2005.

LAGARDÈRE, Geneviève, and ROUSSET-CHARNU, Gérard, *Les Quatre Saisons de Carmontelle. Divertissement et illusions au siècle des Lumières*, Somogy, Éditions d'Art, 2008. Work published for the exhibition "Le Voyage en images de Carmontelle, divertissement et illusions au siècle des Lumières" (Sceaux, Musée d'Île-de-France, 17 April–18 August 2008)

PASTI AUX-THIRIAT, Georgette, et PASTI AUX, Jean, *Un créateur de papiers peints, Joseph Dufour, 1754–1827*, Tramayes (Saône-et-Loire), 2000.

PETIT, Eugène-Claudius (ed.), *Trois Siècles de papier peint*, Paris, Union centrale des arts décoratifs, June–October 1967.

Papiers peints à l'Exposition universelle de 1900 à Paris, Imprimerie nationale, Paris, 1901.

Exposition internationale des arts décoratifs et industriels modernes, Paris, 1925, Section artistique et technique, General report.

Deux Siècles de costumes et de papiers peints. Collections du château-musée de Blois et du musée du Papier peint de Rixheim, Blois, 22 December 1989–25 February 1990, Rixheim, 8 June–1 October 1990, *Ville de Blois et Musée du Papier peint de Rixheim*.

Le Murmure des murs. Quatre siècles d'histoire du papier peint, Bruxelles, galerie CGER, 21 February–18 May 1997.

Thomas Couture, Jules Desfossé. Souper à la Maison d'Or, Musée de l'Hôtel du Vermandois, Senlis, Musée des Arts décoratifs, 1998.

Le Bon Motif. Papiers peints et tissus. Les trésors de la bibliothèque Forney, 1760–1960, September–December 2004, Paris, Bibliothèques Éditions, 2004.

Papiers peints du XXᵉ siècle, Musée du Papier peint, Rixheim, 5 April 2003–1 October 2004.

Musée Galliera, *Exposition historique de l'aéronautique et rétrospective du papier peint : catalogue : novembre 1933-janvier 1934*, Paris, Frazier-Soye.

MUSEUM CATALOGS IN ENGLISH

LYNN, Catherine, *Wallpaper in the Collection of Cooper-Hewitt Museum*, Smithsonian Institution, Eastern Press, 1981.

OMAN, Charles, *Catalogue of Wallpapers, Victoria and Albert Museum*, The Board of Education, University Press, Edinburgh, 1929.

Historic Wallpapers in the Whitworth Art Gallery, Whitworth Art Gallery, 1972.

MUSEUM CATALOGS IN FRENCH

GUIBERT, Mireille, *Papiers peints, 1800-1875*, Société des amis de la bibliothèque Forney, Paris, Les Presses artistiques, 1980.

JACQUÉ, Bernard, *Le Papier peint, décor d'illusion*, Barembach, Éditions Jean-Pierre Gyss, 2nd edition, 1989.

JACQUÉ, Bernard (ed.), *Les Papiers peints en arabesques*, Paris, Éditions de La Martinière, 1995.

MESSINGER, Sylvie (ed.), *Dominos, papiers imprimés*, Paris, Réunion des musées nationaux, 1991.

MESSINGER, Sylvie (ed.), *Bordures et frises, papiers peints*, Paris, Réunion des musées nationaux, 1991.

MESSINGER, Sylvie (ed.), *Fleurs et motifs*, Paris, Réunion des musées nationaux, 1991.

NOUVEL, Odile, *Papiers peints français, 1800-1850*, Fribourg, Office du Livre, 1981.

MUSEUM CATALOGS IN GERMAN

MICK Ernst Wolfgang, *Deutsches Tapetenmuseum*, Kassel, Verlag Thiele & Schwarz, Kassel – Wilhelmshöhe, 1983.

THÜMMLER, Sabine, *Die Geschichte der Tapete – Raumkunst aus Papier*, Aus den Beständen des Deutschen Tapetenmuseum Kassel, Staatliche Museen Kassel, Minerva Hermann Farnung, Eurasburg, 1998.

THÜMMLER, Sabine, *Tapetenkunst, Französische Raumgestaltung und Innendekoration von 1730-1960*, Staatliche Museen Kassel, Éditions Minerva Hermann Farnung, Wolfratshausen, 2000.

Papiertapeten - Bestände, Erhaltung und Restaurierung, Staatliche Schlösser, Burgen und Gärten Sachsen, und Landesamt für Denkmalpflege Sachsen, Michel Sandstein Verlag, Dresden 2005.

ARTICLES

CERMAN, Jérémie, "Wallpaper in the Berges House near Grenoble: from Eclecticism to Art Nouveau", *Studies in the Decorative Arts*, vol. 13, no 1, automne-hiver 2005-2006, The Bard Graduate Center for Studies in the Decorative Arts, Design and Culture, New York, 2005.

JACQUÉ, Bernard, "Wallpaper in the Royal Apartments at the Tuileries, 1789-1792", *Studies in the Decorative Arts*, vol. 13, no 1, Fall-Winter 2005-2006, The Bard Graduate Center for Studies in the Decorative Arts, Design and Culture, New York, 2005.

THÜMMLER, Sabine, "The Battle of Austerlitz Scenic Wallpaper: New Dating and Old Politics", *Studies in the Decorative Arts*, vol. 4, no 2, Spring–Summer 1997, The Bard Graduate Center for Studies in the Decorative Arts, Design and Culture, New York, 1997.

MUSEUMS AND INSTITUTIONS HOUSING IMPORTANT WALLPAPER COLLECTIONS

MUSÉE DES ARTS DÉCORATIFS, PARIS

The wallpaper collection in the Musée des Arts Décoratifs in Paris is considered the finest in the world, with over three hundred thousand items dating from the seventeenth century to the present. The museum opened in 1905, subsequent to the founding, in 1882, of the Union Centrale des Arts Décoratifs (UCAD). Its collection derives basically from private initiatives, namely donations and bequests by decorative-art industrialists who wished to display and preserve France's heritage. Wallpaper entered the collection right from the start, benefiting from support by manufacturers such as Desfossé & Karth, Truquetil, and Zuber, as well as designer Poterlet. Regular gifts and purchases—notably part of the large Follot collection and the entire archives of the Leroy firm—constantly enriched the collection. Furthermore, the museum boasts a large selection of scenic wallpapers.[1] A special department of wallpapers within the museum was created in 1967 for a show titled *Trois Siècles de Papier Peint* (Three Centuries of Wallpaper). The aim of this department, like all the other decorative arts in the museum's collection, is to enlighten designers and decorative artists by providing them with models, thereby "sustaining in France an artistic culture that seeks to create the beautiful within the useful."[2]

Collaborating closely with well-known manufacturers, the museum is actively interested in contemporary design, in the constantly evolving trends and fashions in wallpaper.

A selection of wallpapers has been on permanent display since the revamping and reopening of the museum in 2006. Consultation and presentation of the extremely rich collection can be done by appointment with the curator, Véronique de la Hougue.

MUSÉE DU PAPIER PEINT, RIXHEIM, FRANCE

This museum, which opened in Alsace in 1983, is the only one in France solely devoted to wallpaper. It has a large collection of nearly thirty thousand items, initially constituted from the stock of the Zuber factory in Rixheim, founded in 1790 and still doing business today. The collection has grown beyond Zuber's own output, since it now includes part of the Follot collection as well as important *dominos* and wallpapers from the eighteenth century. The museum has an active, varied acquisition policy. One area is reserved for the presentation of manufacturing techniques. Every year Bernard Jacqué, the curator of the museum, organizes a themed exhibition and regularly publishes catalogues and other documents in conjunction with archivist Philippe de Fabry.

BIBLIOTHÈQUE FORNEY, PARIS

This public library was founded in 1886 thanks to a bequest made to the City of Paris by Aimé Samuel Forney, heir to a family of cabinet-makers.

Its goal being to promote the arts and crafts, the library was initially located on Rue Titon, in the Faubourg Saint-Antoine district where many wallpaper manufacturers operated (notably the famous Réveillon premises, known as La Folie-Titon). The Bibliothèque Forney originally focused on acquiring technical books and catalogues on the crafts, aimed at professionals and students, and it soon had the largest collection in France. In addition to that specialty, the library also holds posters, postcards, wallpapers and textiles. Its remarkable collection of wallpapers was launched and consolidated by its own curator and expert, Henri Clouzot, from 1908 to 1920. In 1914 he founded a "friends' association" (Société des Amis de la Bibliothèque Forney) that included industrialists such as Félix and Charles Follot and Lucien Le Mardelé, who helped to develop the collection. Today it boasts one of the large and most interesting collections with over eight thousand items dating from 1760 to 1960, notably including sets by Dufour & Leroy and Desfossé & Karth, plus a remarkable selection of fragments and samples from the nineteenth century and the art nouveau and art deco periods.[3] The library moved to the Hôtel de Sens in central Paris in 1961; the current curator is Dominique Deangeli-Cayol.

CABINET DES ESTAMPES, BIBLIOTHÈQUE NATIONALE, PARIS

The collection in the print department (Cabinet des Estampes) of the Bibliothèque Nationale is based on copyright-protection deposits made between 1798 and 1802: an exceptional set of papers has been conserved in an extremely fresh state. These wallpapers include designs by makers such as Legrand, Simon, La Veuve Dutoit, Dusserre, Jacquemart, and Bénard.

DEUTSCHES TAPETENMUSEUM, KASSEL, GERMANY

Like the Rixheim museum, the Deutsches Tapetenmuseum in Germany is solely devoted to wallpaper. It was founded in 1923 by dealer Gustav Iven. Its collection originated from donations by various wallpaper manufacturers and merchants. Since it was founded, the museum has moved into other types of wall covering, including Renaissance and baroque leathers, especially gilded leather, as well as eighteenth-century fabric linings. The collection retraces the history of wallpaper from its origin to the twentieth century, featuring a large selection of German products as well as a few magnificent French pieces thanks to its purchase of the Bernard Poteau collection. It also has an interesting selection of the finest twentieth-century designers. The curator is Sabine Thummler.

VICTORIA & ALBERT MUSEUM, LONDON

The wallpaper collection of the Victoria & Albert Museum (V&A) dates back to 1843–51 for items from the School of Design and to 1852 for the Department of Practical Art at Marlborough House. These two institutions merged to become the South Kensington Museum, later named the V&A.

Originally, wallpaper was part of the decorative-arts department. Then in 1909 it was attached to the department of prints and drawings, which in 2000 merged with the National Art Library and the Archive of Art & Design to become the Word & Image Department. Today the V&A's wallpaper collection contains approximately ten thousand items. Some are on show in the permanent display, others appear occasionally in temporary exhibitions devoted to wallpaper. The collection's strong point is English wallpaper of all periods. Much of the collection can be consulted in the Prints & Drawings Study Room. The curator is Gill Saunders.

WHITWORTH ART GALLERY, UNIVERSITY OF MANCHESTER

The largest collection of wallpapers in England after the V&A in London is held by the Whitworth Art Gallery in Manchester. Equal in quality to the best European and American institutions, the collection is based on a 1967 bequest by Wall Paper Manufacturers, Ltd. Enriched by other gifts and purchases, the collection now covers the period from the seventeenth century to the present, focusing on English output but including splendid French and European pieces. In 1984 the gallery created a special wallpaper department and appointed a curator. The Whitworth Art Gallery launched the Wallpaper History Society and maintains close links with the wallpaper industry and contemporary design and creation. Regular exhibitions are organized around the collection. Specialists and researchers can examine wallpapers by appointment with the curator, Christine Woods.

COOPER-HEWITT NATIONAL DESIGN MUSEUM, NEW YORK

The museum's roots go back to the founding of the Cooper Union for the Advancement of Sciences & Art in New York in 1859 by businessman and art-lover Peter Cooper. This free college notably aimed to train young artists and designers. In 1897 a sister museum was founded, the Cooper Union Museum for the Arts & Decoration. Its founders, Sarah and Eleanor Hewitt, built up a major collection of engravings, drawings, textiles and wallpapers, numbering over 100,000 items. In 1967, after experiencing a long period of crisis, the museum was saved largely due to the efforts of patron and collector

Henry F. Du Pont (founder of the Winterthur Museum). It was placed under the aegis of the Smithsonian Institution in Washington, but remained in New York, where it moved into the elegant Andrew Carnegie Mansion on Fifth Avenue: in 1979, the Cooper - Hewitt National Design Museum officially opened its doors to the public. Its collection of wallpaper is the largest and finest in the United States, with over ten thousand items, half of which focus on twentieth-century America (notably the Nancy McClelland archives); one-third of the collection is French production from the eighteenth to the first half of the nineteenth century, the remaining items being English, German, Italian, and Chinese in origin. Over the years the museum has organized various exhibitions on wallpaper, such as *Rooms with a View: Landscape and Wallpaper*, held from April to October, 2001. Today the Cooper - Hewitt National Design Museum is one of the best sources for studying wallpaper and design; the curator is Gregory Herringshaw.

RHODE ISLAND SCHOOL OF DESIGN

Founded in 1877, the Rhode Island School of Design (RISD) is now one of the finest art and design schools in the United States. Its museum of European and American decorative arts includes a collection of wallpaper featuring eighteenth- and nineteenth-century French examples based on the 1935 purchase of the Mr. and Mrs. Charles Huard collection of over five hundred items. The museum is particularly active in promoting contemporary design, as witnessed by its 2003 show, *On the Wall*.

WINTERTHUR MUSEUM, DELAWARE

This museum, founded by art-lover Henry F. Du Pont, boasts one of the finest collections of American decorative arts. Du Pont also became interested in European and Chinese wallpapers in the 1920s, when they were all the rage. The museum's period rooms thus feature Réveillon paper once in the Phelps-Hatheway House and the Chinese paper from the Huard collection, purchased through Nancy McClelland. The wallpaper collection is part of the museum's prints and paintings department, curated by Anne Verplanck.

HISTORIC NEW ENGLAND SOCIETY FOR THE PRESERVATION OF NEW ENGLAND ANTIQUITIES

This preservation society serves as an umbrella organization for a group of residences labeled "Historic New England Homes" that still contain, in situ, examples of some of the finest American, English, and French wallpapers to be found in the United States. The Society has the oldest and largest documentation and study center in the country, focusing on the relationship between architecture and interior decoration. The curator is Richard Nylander.

Notes

1. These papers were featured in the exhibition, *Décors de l'imaginaire, papiers peints panoramiques, 1790-1865*, September 1990–January 1991.
2. Yvonne Brunhammer, *Le Beau dans l'utile: Un musée pour les arts décoratifs* (Paris: Gallimard, 1992), p. 11.
3. These items were featured in the exhibition, *Le Bon Motif: Papiers peints et tissus, Les trésors de la Bibliothèque Forney, 1760–1960*, September–December 2004.